# THE EVIDENCE ROOM

# THE EVIDENCE ROOM

Anne Bordeleau
Sascha Hastings
Donald McKay
Robert Jan van Pelt

NEW JEWISH PRESS

This edition published in 2016 by
New Jewish Press
Anne Tanenbaum Centre for Jewish Studies
University of Toronto
170 St. George Street, Room 218
Toronto, Ontario M5R 2M8
www.newjewishpress.ca

Editor: Sascha Hastings
Designer: Louis-Charles Lasnier
Production: Jolin Masson


Library and Archives Canada Cataloguing in Publication
The evidence room / Anne Bordeleau, Sascha Hastings,
    Donald McKay, Robert Jan van Pelt.

Includes bibliographical references.
ISBN 978-1-988326-00-9 (hardback)

1. Auschwitz (Concentration camp)–Buildings. 2. Concentration camp buildings–
    Poland–Design and construction. 3. Holocaust, Jewish (1939-1945), and
    architecture. 4. Irving, David John Cawdell, 1938- –Trials, litigation, etc.
    5. Lipstadt, Deborah E.–Trials, litigation, etc. 6. Penguin (Firm)–Trials, litiga-
    tion, etc. 7. Trials (Libel)–England–London. 8. Holocaust denial. 9. Holocaust,
    Jewish (1939-1945)–Historiography. I. Bordeleau, Anne, 1972- . Casts court.

D805.5.A96E95 2016        940.53'18        C2016-902107-6


First Edition
10 9 8 7 6 5 4 3 2 1

Printed and bound in Canada by Maracle Press

In memory of Henryk Tauber Fuchsbrunner (1917–2000),
for his invaluable 1945 testimony on the design and operation
of the Auschwitz gas chambers.

The following images are some of the evidence successfully used in a 2000 London libel suit to challenge the false assertion by a revisionist historian and Holocaust denier that there had been no gas chambers in Auschwitz and that therefore the Holocaust didn't happen. These images were also used to research and produce the plaster casts presented in *The Evidence Room* exhibition, hence the varied provenance and image quality. Captions may be found on pp. 154–161.

fig. 1

fig. 2

fig. 3

fig. 4

fig. 5

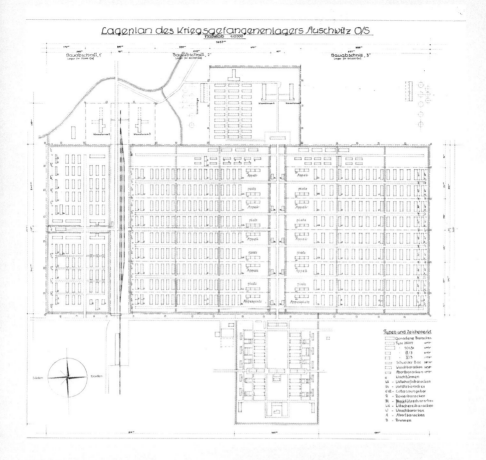

fig. 6

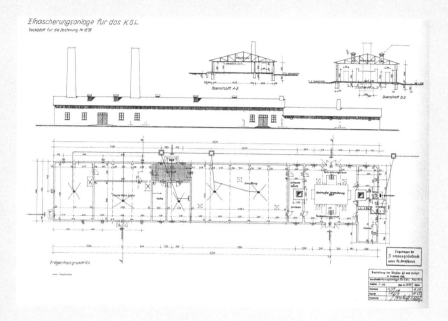

fig. 7

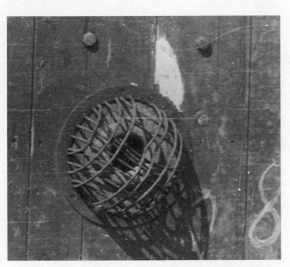

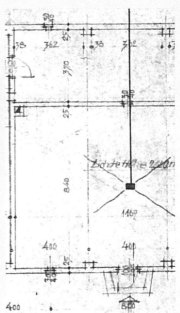

fig. 8                              fig. 9

fig. 10

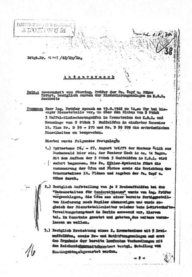

Bftgb.Nr. 41445 /42/Er/La.

A k t e n v e r m e r k

Betr.: Anwesenheit von Obering. Prüfer der Fa. Topf u. Söhne
Erfurt, bezüglich Ausbau der Einäscherungsanlagen im K.G.L.
Auschwitz

Vorgang: Herr Ing. Prüfer sprach am 19.8.1942 um 14.oo Uhr bei hiesiger Dienststelle vor, um über den Einbau von 5 Stück
3 Muffel-Einäscherungsöfen in Krematorium des K.G.L. und
Neuanlage von 2 Stück 3 Muffelöfen in einfacher Bauweise
lt. Plan Nr. D 59 - 970 und Nr. D 59 999 die erforderlichen
Einzelheiten zu besprechen.

Hierbei wurde folgendes festgelegt:

1.) Spätestens 26. - 27. August trifft der Monteur Kolik aus
Buchenwald hier ein, der Monteur Koch in ca. 14 Tagen.
Mit dem Aufbau der 5 Stück 3 Muffelöfen im K.G.L. wird
sofort begonnen. Die Fa. Kähler-Myslowitz führt die
Ausmauerung der Öfen und Fuchse sowie die Errichtung des
Schornsteines lt. Plänen und Angaben der Fa. Topf u.
Söhne durch.

2.) Bezüglich Aufstellung von je 2 Dreimuffelöfen bei den
"Badeanstalten für Sonderaktionen" wurde von Ing. Prüfer
vorgeschlagen, die Öfen aus einer bereits fertiggestellten Lieferung nach Mogilew abzunehmen und wurde sogleich der Dienststellenleiter welcher beim ß-Wirtschaftsverwaltungshauptamt in Berlin anwesend war, hiervon
tel. in Kenntnis gesetzt und gebeten, das weitere veranlassen zu wollen.

3.) Bezüglich Errichtung eines 2. Krematoriums mit 5 Dreimuffelöfen, sowie Be- und Entlüftungsanlagen muß erst
das Ergebnis der bereits laufenden Verhandlungen mit
den Reichsministerium....tehauptamt bestätigt, Zuteilung von
Kontingenten abgewartet werden.

- 2 -

fig. 12                                          fig. 13

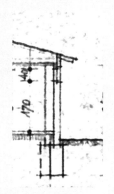

fig. 14

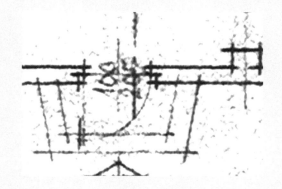

fig. 15

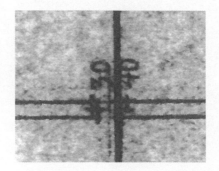

fig. 16

fig. 17

fig. 18

fig. 19

fig. 20

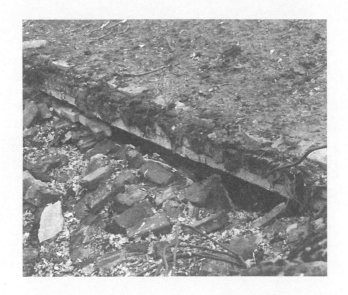

fig. 21

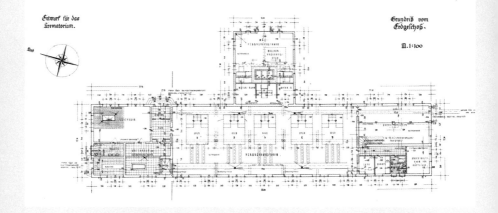

fig. 22

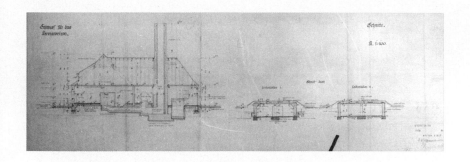

fig. 23

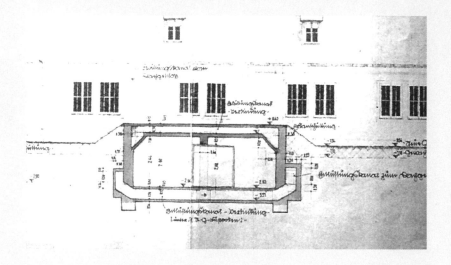

fig. 24

fig. 25

fig. 26

31550/Ja./No.-

Betr.: Fertigstellung d. Krematoriums III
Bezug: ohne
Anl.: -/-

An das
SS-Wirtschafts-Verwaltungs-
hauptamt.Amtsgruppenchef C
SS-Brigadeführer u.Generalmajor
Dr.-Ing. K a m m l e r
Berlin- Lichterfelde.- West.

Unter den Zeichen 126 - 135

Melde die Fertigstellung des Krematoriums III mit dem
26.6.1943.Mithin sind sämtliche befohlenen Krematorien fertiggestellt.

Leistung der nunmehr vorhandenen Krematorien
bei einer 24 stündigen Arbeitszeit :

1.) altes Krematorium I
    3 x 2 Muffelöfen                              340    Personen
2.) neues Krematorium i.K.G.L. II
    5 x 3 Muffelöfen                             1440    Personen
3.) neues Krematorium III
    5 x 3 Muffelöfen                             1440    Personen
4.) neues Krematorium IV.
    8      Muffelöfen                             768    Personen
5.) neues Krematorium V.
    8      Muffelöfen                             768    Personen

Insges.bei 24 stündiger Arbeitszeit             4756    Personen

Verteiler:                          Der Leiter der Zentralbauleitung
A1 -                                der Waffen-SS und Polizei Auschwitz
   - Kirschnek
Registratur K.G.L. BW. 30

                                    SS-Sturmbannführer.

22957/43/Jäh/Fm.

Betr.: Krematorium III- K.G.L.-Auschwitz- O/S.
Bezug: Telegramm der Zentralbauleitung Auschwitz
        vom 10.2.1943 - 2o,o5 Uhr.-
Anlg.: - - -


Firma
J.A. T o p f & S ö h n e
Maschinenfabrik

E r f u r t
Dreyaestrasse 7/9

Mit o.a. Telegramm wurde der bereits getätigte Auftrag der gesamten Maschineneinrichtungen einschl.2 Stck.endgültigen e-
lektrischen Leichenaufzügen und 1 provisorischen,kurzfristig
lieferbaren Leichenaufzug,sowie einer praktischen Kohlenbe-
schickungs- und Aschentransportvorrichtung nochmals bestätigt.
Sie haben daher die Anlage K III kompl.zu liefern und zu er-
stellen.Es wird erwartet,dass nunmehr alles daran gesetzt wird,
damit die gesamten Maschinenteile sofort fertiggestellt werden
und zum Versand kommen.
Die Inbetriebnahme der Gesamtanlage muß bestimmt am 1o.April
1943 erfolgen.
Die Zentralbauleitung erwartet,daß Sie mit der Einhaltung des
Termins bei dieser Anlage die Scharten wieder auswetzen,welche
durch Nichterfüllen von Versprechungen und mehrmalige Schrei-
ben,die nicht den Tatsachen entsprachen,bei den Lieferungen
der Öfen für Krem.II.K.G.L.entstanden.So schrieben Sie am
21.1.1943,daß die gesamten Materialien für die Be- und Entlüf-
tungsanlage am 22.1.43 zum Versand kommen.Beim Eintreffen des
Waggons fehlten diese Teile,sodaß Ihr Monteur Messing nicht
weiter konnte.Am Telefon sagte Ihr Herr Prüfer,daß sämtliche
Materialien abgegangen seien.Bei nochmaliger Reklamierung wurde

- 2 -

---

- 2 -

von einem anderen Herrn mitgeteilt,daß die restlichen Materiali-
en noch nicht fertig seien.Zum Schluß waren dann die fertiggestellten Materialien angeblich im Lager gestapelt worden.
Jetzt geht ein Frachtbrief ein mit Versandanzeige vom 6.2.1943.
Nach Prüfung desselben und Rücksprache mit Ihren Monteur wird
festgestellt,daß ein Gebläse Nr. 450 mit 3.5 PS-Motor wieder
fehlt und ausgerechnet das Gebläse für L.-Keller I,welches am
dringendsten benötigt wird. Außerdem 1 Motor 7,5 PS für das Ab-
luftgebläse Nr. 550 für L-Keller II.
Es wurde Ihnen deshalb wieder telegraphiert:"Absendet sofort
auf Versandanzeige 6.2.43 nicht angegebenes Gebläse 450
mit 3,5 PS-Motor für L-Keller I und Motor 7,5 PS für Abluftge-
bläse Nr.550 für L-Keller II, da andernfalls Anlage nicht in
Betrieb genommen werden kann.Drahtantwort."
Dafoh diese Vernachlässigungen Ihrerseits entstehen der Zentralbauleitung die größten Schwierigkeiten.Sie werden deshalb er-
sucht,sofort die fehlenden Materialien per Eilgut zum Versand
zu bringen,damit endlich die Anlage fertiggestellt wird.

                    Der Leiter der Zentralbauleitung
                    der Waffen-SS und Polizei Auschwitz
                         gez.Bischoff
                         SS-Sturmbannführer.

Verteiler:
1 Sachbearbeiter Jähring
1 SS-Ustuf.Janisch
1 SS-Ustuf.Kirschneck
1 Registratur (Akt:BW.30.-Krematorium)

F.d.R.d.A.
gez.Unterschrift
SS-Untersturmführer(H)

F.d.R.d.A.
Prüfer
17.7.1941

fig. 29

Tgb.: 11/16/43/Swo/Lm          Auschwitz, am 29.1.1943

A k t e n v e r m e r k
_____

Betr.: Stromversorgung und Installation des KL und KGL.

       Besprechung am 29.1.43 zwischen Zentralbauleitung
Auschwitz und AEG-Kattowitz, Anwesende:
       Ing. Tomitschek - AEG und
       SS-Uscha. Swoboda - Zentralbauleitung.
       Die AEG teilt mit, dass ihr auf ihre Eisen- und Metall-
anforderung, welche teilweise schon im November 1942 ausge-
schrieben wurden, bisher noch keine gültigen Eisen- und Metallscheine zur Verfügung gestellt wurden. Es war dieser Firma
aus diesem Grunde bisher nicht möglich, die bestellten
Anlageteile in Arbeit zu nehmen. Es besteht die grosse Ge-
fahr, dass durch weitere Verzögerung in der Kontingentierung
dieser Aufträge die Liefertermine wesentlich verlängert werden.
       Aus diesem Grunde ist es auch nicht möglich, die In-
stallation und Stromversorgung des Krematoriums II im KGL
bis 31.1.43 fertigzustellen. Das Krematorium kann lediglich
aus baulichen, für andere Bauten bestimmten Materialien so-
weit fertiggestellt werden, dass eine Inbetriebsetzung frühe-
stens am 15.2.43 erfolgen kann. Diese Inbetriebsetzung kann
sich jedoch nur auf beschränkten Gebrauch der vorhandenen
Maschinen erstrecken (wobei eine Verbrennung mit gleichzeitiger
Sonderbehandlung möglich gemacht wird), da die zum Krematorium führende Zuleitung für dessen Leistungsverbrauch zu
schwach ist. Für das hierfür erforderliche Freileitungs-
material sind ebenfalls noch keine Eisen- und Metallscheine
zugewiesen worden.
       Eine Stromversorgung des Krematoriums III ist aus
vorgenannten Gründen derzeit überhaupt nicht möglich.

..............                    ..............
Vertreter der AEG               SS-Unterscharführer
z.K.g.

SS-Hauptsturmführer

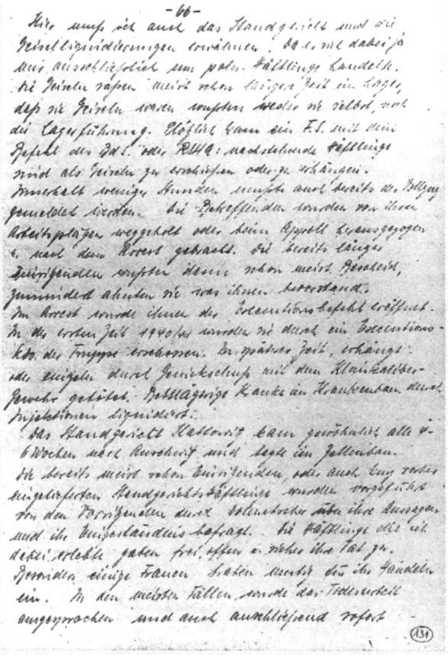

-66-

Hier muß ich auch das Standgericht und die Geisel-Liquidierungen erwähnen, da es sich dabei ja auch ausschließlich um poln. Häftlinge handelt. Die Geiseln saßen meist schon längere Zeit im Lager, daß sie Geiseln waren wußten weder sie selbst, noch die Lagerführung. Plötzlich kam ein F.S. mit dem Befehl des Bd.S. oder RSHA: nachstehende Häftlinge sind als Geiseln zu erschießen oder zu erhängen. Innerhalb weniger Stunden mußte auch bereits der Vollzug gemeldet werden. Die Betreffenden wurden von ihren Arbeitsplätzen weggeholt oder beim Appell herausgezogen u. nach dem Arrest gebracht. Die bereits länger Einsitzenden wußten schon meist Bescheid, zumindest ahnten sie was ihnen bevorstand. Im Arrest wurde ihnen der Exekutionsbefehl eröffnet. In der ersten Zeit 1940/41 wurden sie durch ein Exekutions-Kdo. der Truppe erschossen. In späterer Zeit, erhängt oder einzeln durch Genickschuß mit dem Kleinkaliber-Gewehr getötet. Bettlägerige Kranke im Krankenbau durch Injektionen liquidiert.

Das Standgericht Kattowitz kam gewöhnlich alle 4–6 Wochen nach Auschwitz und tagte im Zellenbau. Die bereits meist schon Einsitzenden, oder auch kurz vorher eingelieferten Standgerichtshäftlinge wurden vorgeführt, von dem Vorsitzenden durch Dolmetscher über ihre Aussagen und ihr Geständnis befragt. Die Häftlinge die ich dabei erlebte gaben frei, offen u. sicher ihre Tat zu. Besonders einige Frauen traten mutig für ihr Handeln ein. In den meisten Fällen wurde das Todesurteil ausgesprochen und auch anschließend sofort

131

fig. 31

fig. 32

fig. 33

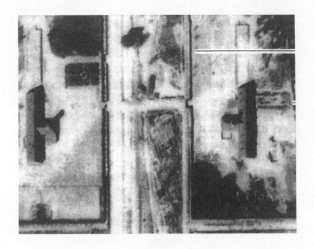

fig. 34

fig. 35

fig. 36

fig. 37

fig. 38

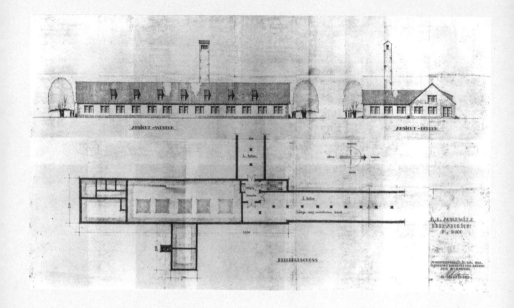

fig. 39

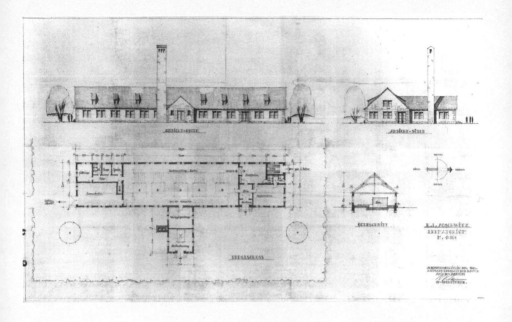

fig. 40

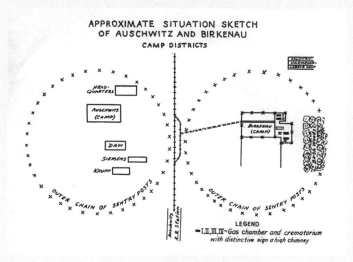

fig. 41

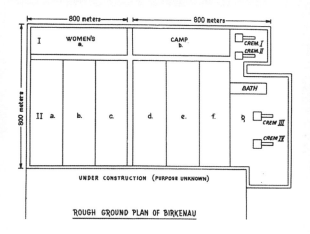

ROUGH GROUND PLAN OF BIRKENAU

fig. 42

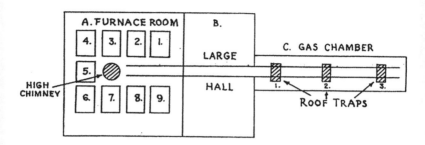

ROUGH GROUND PLAN OF
CREMATORIA: TYPES I & II IN BIRKENAU

fig. 43

fig. 44

fig. 45

fig. 46

fig. 47

fig. 48

fig. 49

fig. 50

fig. 51

fig. 52

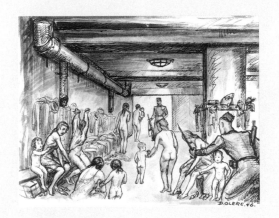

fig. 53

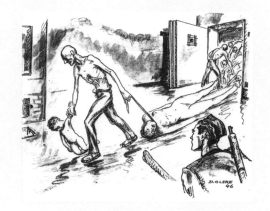

fig. 54

fig. 55

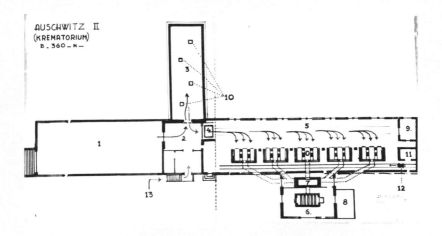

fig. 56

fig. 57

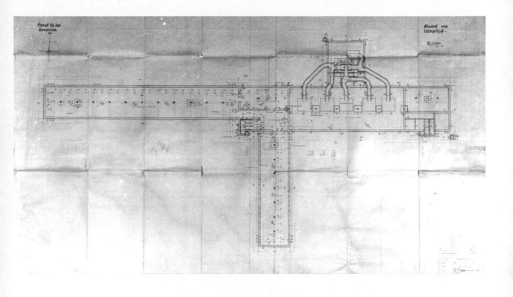

fig. 58

_Krematorium im K.G.L._

Deckblatt zu Zeichnung № 932 u. 933,
Verlegung des Kellerzuganges an die Strassenseite,

Kellergeschoss

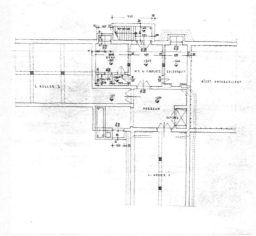

fig. 59

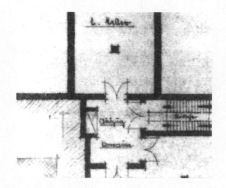

fig. 60

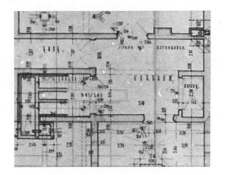 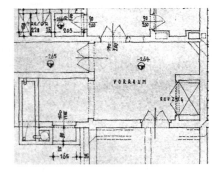

fig. 61                    fig. 62

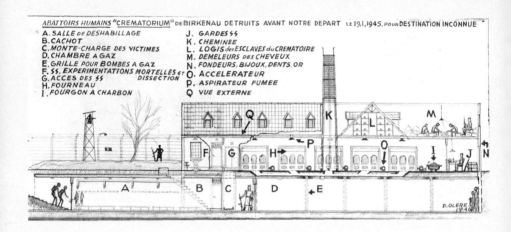

fig. 63

# Table of Contents

*The Evidence Room* Project
– Elly Gotz

Today I touched the gas column—a reproduction of the device that inserted Zyklon-B into the gas chambers at Auschwitz.

As a Holocaust survivor I felt the cold hand of history on my spine.

I knew a good deal about the Auschwitz-Birkenau murder factory, but the gas column really shocked me. Because of what I had read about people thinking they were going into a shower room, I had always imagined the gas being dispersed by sprinklers. Touching that construction had a profound effect on me—a new visceral recognition, all these years later.

The gas column was in the workshop at the University of Waterloo School of Architecture where a team of professors and students is preparing a remarkable exhibition destined for the Venice Architecture Biennale in May 2016.

The exhibition creates a visual and tactile impression of the forensic architectural evidence presented by expert defense witness Professor Robert Jan van Pelt at the 2000 trial in London for Holocaust denier David Irving's suit against historian Deborah Lipstadt and her publisher for libel. The truth of the Holocaust became the issue in contention.

A major element of the display is a reconstruction of the steel mesh gas column through which Zyklon-B gas pellets were lowered into the gas chamber. The display also includes reproductions in plaster-cast relief of original architectural drawings for the construction of Auschwitz-Birkenau, the door of the gas chamber with a tight seal around the edge and a hinged lid covering the exterior peephole, and other artifacts.

The whole exhibition will be white, the only thing to separate our present reality from the monstrous artifacts at hand, perhaps to permit us to remain unsoiled by the black reality of the evil it represents.

For me, a survivor of Dachau, the most compelling feature of the exhibition is its tactile character. By removing colour, sound, and interpretation from *The Evidence Room*, we are forced to rely on touch to elicit its meaning. Most people are by now aware of the Holocaust. It is possible to know things, to be aware of them, but not feel them. This exhibition lets people touch the metal of the gas column, run their fingers over the drawings, and connect in that mysterious way that sometimes happens when reality overwhelms us by becoming part of us.

It is difficult to imagine the details of a gas chamber, where humans were locked in to die. One has to feel the double grates that protected the bucket filled with poison pellets from the desperate hands of the condemned, peer into the bucket, and imagine the pellets melting away, the poison oozing out of them. Only then can real awareness arise in the soul and place the viewer INSIDE the gas chamber.

The simplicity of this killing machine is obscene. I imagine the designers, engineers, and architects congratulating themselves on such a cheap and cunning solution.

Today's visit is still reverberating with me. I'm still processing what I saw and felt.


February 23, 2016

The Evidence in the Room and the Memory of the Offence
– Robert Jan van Pelt

"*Les architectes inventent calmement ces porches destinés à n'être franchis qu'une seule fois*—The architects calmly plan the gates through which no one will enter more than once."[1] I heard these words for the first time in 1974 when, as a freshman, I saw Alain Resnais' film *Nuit et Brouillard* (Night and Fog). Having fallen in love with architecture while visiting the French cathedrals during family holidays, I aimed to become an architectural historian. Nikolaus Pevsner's *An Outline of European Architecture* had been my guide, and that book, which limited its discussion on Nazi architecture to a terse "the less said the better,"[2] had not prepared me for the simple fact, noted in the first minute of *Nuit et Brouillard*, that architects, professional architects, had designed factories of death like Auschwitz.

It took a decade for that seed of a thought to germinate into an awareness that the five gas-chamber-equipped crematoria of Auschwitz might be as important to our understanding of architecture as the great cathedrals of the Île-de-France. Two buildings bridged the abyss between Chartres and Auschwitz. My mentor, the great Renaissance scholar, Dame Frances Yates, author of *The Art of Memory* (1966) and *Theatre of the World* (1969), introduced me to the concept of a building as a vessel of memory, most perfectly exemplified in Giulio Camillo's Theatre of Memory, a room filled with images that allowed the visitor to "at once perceive with his eyes everything that is otherwise hidden in the depths of the human mind."[3] She also inspired me to study the Temple of Solomon as *imago mundi*, or image of the world. A moment of epiphany came during my PhD defence, when one of my examiners asked me if I thought there was any building today that rivalled the Temple of Solomon in importance. I was unprepared for the question, and without really having had a chance to think, said, "Yes. Auschwitz."

A year later, in 1985, I was teaching architectural history at a prestigious American university. Attending a faculty meeting to discuss the 750 buildings that doctoral students were to know for their comprehensive exam, I suggested we include not only Camillo's Theatre and Solomon's Temple, but also Auschwitz Crematorium 2—the most deadly building in that camp. A stunned silence was finally broken by one professor's acid observation that I must be joking. Another suggested I find an alternative career. Instead I found another home for my work in Canada at the University of Waterloo School of Architecture. The reason was simple: *Nuit et Brouillard* was already a fixture in the first-year curriculum.

It wasn't until 1989, when the Berlin Wall fell, that I began to study the thousands of architectural blueprints and construction documents tracking the building of Auschwitz, including the crematoria, preserved in European archives—most importantly the one in the

Auschwitz Museum. The documents allowed me to reconstruct, in detail, the cavalier manner in which SS architects like Karl Bischoff (never indicted), and Fritz Ertl and Walter Dejaco (both tried and acquitted in 1972) had designed the camp without any regard for the inmates' health: a special find was a blueprint of a barrack containing a handwritten calculation that, on the basis of assuming four instead of three inmates per bunk, increased the capacity of the building from roughly 550 to 744 inmates. The documents showed at times remarkable levels of incompetence, but they revealed the step-by-step approach that had led to the construction of buildings like Crematorium 2 that was to serve the purpose of genocide by means of a spacious undressing room, a large underground homicidal cyanide gas chamber offering standing room to 2,000 people, a corpse elevator, and fifteen high-capacity ovens with an official daily capacity of 1,440 corpses (the total daily incineration capacity of the four crematoria in Auschwitz-Birkenau was 4,416 corpses). However my aim was not forensic: I tried to understand the history of Auschwitz as a historian, not as a detective, prosecutor, or advocate. My primary focus was on questions of interpretation, not on those of fact or evidence.

Yet from the beginning of my research, I realized that the forensic significance of the architectural documentation of the Auschwitz crematoria continued to be relevant despite the fact that, by the late 1980s, any future trials of Auschwitz SS personnel, like those of 1947 (Krakow), 1963–67 (Frankfurt), and 1972 (Vienna) seemed unlikely. I had begun to encounter the writings of Holocaust deniers, who maintain that the systematic murder of six million Jews never happened, that the story of the Holocaust is a hoax created and peddled by Jews to libel the Germans, to defraud them out of billions of marks and deprive the Palestinians of a homeland. The great majority of these negationists are antisemites who know very well that the genocide occurred, but take a perverse pleasure in both erasing the victims from the record of history and destroying the innocence of the survivors by turning them into the perpetrators of a massive libel and swindle.

The focus of almost all these Holocaust deniers has been Auschwitz. Indeed, for all practical purposes it is fair to say that Holocaust denial is Auschwitz denial—that is, the denial that Auschwitz was an extermination camp designed with genocidal intentions. I became aware of this when, in the early 1990s, I read an article in which the British negationist David Irving characterized Auschwitz as "the biggest weapon" in what he described as the Jewish propaganda campaign against the truth. Auschwitz was "the great battleship" and, following Churchill's 1941 instruction to "Sink the Bismarck," Irving called on other deniers to "Sink the Auschwitz."[4] As a serious student of the history of Auschwitz, I thought such statements irrelevant for my understanding of the place and did my best to ignore them. Yet living in Toronto, I could not help but notice a local connection that intrigued me: Irving's denial was inspired by a sloppy and unscientific forensic report on the architecture of Auschwitz commissioned in 1988 by Toronto Holocaust denier Ernst Zündel (who at that time was standing trial in the District Court of Ontario) and written by Fred Leuchter, a consultant in execution methods to American prison authorities. Leuchter's report claimed that the ruins of the crematoria and the lack of residual cyanide in the walls of the "alleged" gas chambers proved that Auschwitz had not been an extermination camp in which Jews, as well as Roma and Sinti, had been killed en masse by means of cyanide.[5]

Once a respected writer of histories of the Third Reich, Irving had begun to drift in the late 1970s toward what one might label as soft-core Holocaust denial by maintaining that the Holocaust had happened, but that it had been conducted by rogue elements without approval from Hitler. Attending the Toronto trial and hearing Leuchter's testimony on behalf of Zündel, Irving's soft-core denial turned into the hard-core version peddled by French academic Robert Faurisson: not only had the depiction of Auschwitz as a killing centre been a hoax, but so too was the whole of the Holocaust.

Negationists welcomed Irving's endorsement: it was the first one they had received from a person with a reputation as a historian. For the same reason, those fighting Holocaust denial considered it with alarm. In her book *Denying the Holocaust: The Growing Assault on Truth and Memory* (1993), American historian Deborah Lipstadt therefore identified Irving as a very dangerous falsifier of history. In 1996, in a delayed response, Irving decided to sue Lipstadt and her British publisher, Penguin, for libel in the High Court in London. Since English law is biased toward the plaintiff in libel cases, Lipstadt had to prove the truth in her characterization of Irving as, essentially, a liar.

The suit occurred at a pivotal time for Holocaust memory: more and more survivor-witnesses—who between the early 1960s and the 1990s had been crucial in creating global awareness of the Holocaust and its implications for the future of humankind—were dying because of old age. Those concerned about the future of Holocaust memory after the passing of the last generation of survivor-witnesses realized that historians, who conscientiously interpret testimonies and material evidence, would become the primary bearers of both Holocaust memory and history in the future. The London trial provided an opportunity to test this: no survivor-witnesses would be called, only professional historians who would act as expert witnesses. And the key question was not "What happened?" but "How are historians able to determine the facts on the basis of the convergence of eyewitness testimonies, documentary evidence, and physical remains of, for example, extermination camps such as Auschwitz?"

Because Irving had embraced denial after hearing Leuchter's testimony, Lipstadt's lawyers needed to find a way to discredit not only Leuchter's assumptions, forensic methods, and conclusions, but all the efforts of Holocaust deniers (beginning with Faurisson) to distort and negate the evidence that the Auschwitz gas chambers and crematoria had served a genocidal purpose, killing more than 1.1 million human beings, 90 per cent of whom were Jews from many different countries, 7 per cent of whom were non-Jewish Poles, 2 per cent of whom were Roma and Sinti, and 1 per cent of whom were "gentiles" not belonging to the former groups (primarily Russian POWs). And thus I received in early 1998 an invitation to join the case as an expert witness on all matters concerning Auschwitz.[6]

While I had doubts about my ability to withstand what might be many days of cross-examination—I knew well that in common-law jurisdictions, in which a trial is a fierce combat between opposing sides, many expert witnesses leave the witness box with their professional reputation shattered—a three-fold sense of obligation compelled me to join Lipstadt's defence team. Having had a unique opportunity to study the Auschwitz architectural evidence in its broad historical context, I was uniquely qualified to do the job and felt a professional obligation to testify. While the reputations of Irving and Lipstadt were formally at the centre of the case, I realized that the world at large would interpret the trial as a battle about the truth of the Holocaust and, although this was a misperception, it made all the difference. Given the likely fallout of Lipstadt's defeat—headlines such as "The High Court judges evidence about the genocidal use of Auschwitz to be insufficient"—I felt under a moral obligation to put my life's work at stake. Finally I felt a spiritual obligation to the 1.1 million people murdered in Auschwitz.

I prepared an expert report that tried to do two things: critically assess the forensic analysis of Leuchter and other deniers and account for the evidence that is available about the use of Auschwitz as a factory of death. I framed my consideration of the arguments of the deniers within an analysis of negationist epistemology. Deniers typically dismiss all eyewitness evidence as irrelevant, arguing that survivors lied because they were part of the conspiracy and SS men lied because the post-war trials would have been like the Soviet show trials from the 1930s in which defendants, facing no credible evidence of a crime, publicly incriminated themselves. Instead, deniers focus on material evidence—cyanide traces in walls, documents, photos— that cannot protest attempts of manipulation, misconstruction, and falsification. In relation to this category of evidence, deniers routinely either commit the fallacy of negative proof or they try to "turn" the evidence. An example of the first approach is Irving's claim that Auschwitz was not an extermination camp because there are no official German wartime documents that explicitly state that the camp was purposefully conceived and operated as an extermination camp. Leuchter committed the same fallacy when he claimed that the morgues of the crematoria did not function as gas chambers because there are only negligible traces of cyanide in the walls. Neither argument is legitimate because every historian knows that most evidence does not survive and that the reconstruction of any historical event is based on accidentally preserved relics. And Holocaust deniers routinely try to "turn" evidence by arguing that what appears to be clear-cut German wartime evidence attesting to the presence and operation of a genocidal machinery of death has, in fact, a more innocent meaning. For example, that the underground gas chamber of Crematorium 2, equipped with gastight doors, is characterized as a gas-proof air-raid shelter; that the excessive capacity of the Auschwitz ovens can be explained by the Germans' fear of typhus epidemics, and so on.

In my expert report, I dealt with all these issues in great detail, subjecting negationist arguments to detailed forensic analysis. I did the same with the evidence that supported the conclusion that Auschwitz had been an extermination camp. I analyzed eyewitness statements, such as the very detailed account of the gas chamber of Crematorium 2 given in May 1945 by Auschwitz survivor Henryk Tauber, and squared it with documentary evidence produced by the Germans. For example, Tauber stated that the peephole of the wooden gastight doors designed for and manufactured in Auschwitz had a unique detail: a hemi-spherical wire-mesh cover on the inside of the door. Its purpose was to protect the glass from attempts by the victims to break it. This testimony converged with a photo of a gastight door taken in 1945 by Russian forensic investigators and a German letter specifying the construction of that peephole. Another example was a modification in the way the gastight door was hung into the door-frame. The large basement room in Crematorium 2 had first been designed as a morgue and originally the doors into that space opened inward. When the purpose of the room was changed from morgue to gas chamber, architect Dejaco realized that he had to make the door open outward; it would otherwise be impossible for the slave workers charged with removing the corpses to enter the packed gas chamber after the gassing. A final example: the gastight shutters used to close the Zyklon-B introduction holes in the walls of the gas chambers of Crematoria 4 and 5. I showed that the blueprints of these buildings indicate that these shutters measured thirty by forty centimetres (roughly twelve by sixteen inches), that two gastight shutters of such dimensions survive in the Auschwitz Museum, and that eyewitness evidence confirms the use of such shutters and makes clear that the SS men used a small ladder to reach them. And so on. Deciding on presenting an overwhelming amount of evidence against the deniers and in support of the historical facts, my expert report grew to 750 pages.

I submitted my report in June 1999 and seven months later I defended it under cross-examination in the Royal Courts of Justice in London. Irving acted as his own advocate and, in my cross-examination, focused on a very limited category of evidence for the genocidal use of the crematoria, especially Crematorium 2. The centre of his case was an issue that Holocaust deniers summarize in the slogan "No Holes, No Holocaust." It is based on the assumption that the Holocaust centred on Auschwitz, that the most important extermination installation of Auschwitz was Crematorium 2, that the most important part of Crematorium 2 was the gas chamber, and that the essential detail of the gas chamber were four wire-mesh gas columns connected through holes in the roof of the underground gas chambers of Crematoria 2 and 3 to the outside above. These gas columns served as introduction devices for the cyanide into the gas chambers: when the basement gas chamber had been filled with 2,000 victims and the doors were locked, the SS would empty the contents of canisters of the commercial delousing agent Zyklon-B—pellets of absorbent diatomaceous earth soaked in cyanide—into a basket that they then lowered through the holes to the centre of the hollow column. Activated by the body heat of the victims, the cyanide began to degas in the column and the wire-mesh covering allowed it to spread into the rest of the gas chamber without the possibility of interference by the victims. When all victims were dead, the SS would hoist the basket with the still degassing cyanide through the hole and discard the contents on the roof of the gas chamber. This, and the mechanical ventilation of the space for some fifteen minutes, created conditions that allowed the slave workers to open the door and begin clearing the corpses from the gas chamber. The SS dismantled the gas columns in late 1944 and none survives. The major sources of evidence are statements given in 1945 by Tauber and by Michael Kula, a former prisoner who made the gas columns in the camp metal workshop. For deniers their detailed testimonies are, a priori, inadmissible. Ignoring the traditional aphorism "absence of evidence is not evidence of absence," the deniers turn today's absence of the remains of the gas columns in the ruins of the crematoria, and the difficulty in easily identifying the roof holes in the totally ruined slabs that covered the gas chambers, into a proof that the gas chambers of Crematoria 2 and 3 were ordinary morgues and that hence the Holocaust did not happen. "Without holes, no gassings according to the scenario as described by the eye witnesses, without such gassings no reliable eye witnesses, and without reliable eye witnesses no evidence for the Holocaust," negationist Germar Rudolf wrote in 1998, adding, triumphantly, in capitals: "NO HOLES, NO HOLOCAUST."[7]

Irving tried to convince the judge (both sides had agreed to do without a jury) and the press gallery of the validity of this argument, but failed to do so despite the lengthy, almost ritual incantation of the no-holes argument. Declaring the holes in the roof to be the "cardinal linchpin of the Defence in this action," Irving boldy asserted, in a rhetorical flourish, that the apparent absence of holes in the destroyed slab that covered the gas chamber of Crematorium 2 "blows holes in the whole of the gas chamber story."[8]

He also failed to thwart or deflect my attack on Leuchter's report and he failed to sow doubt in the judge's mind on any of the other forensic interpretations I had made. Indeed, the final judgment in the trial—for the defendants—confirmed all of my arguments. More importantly, it confirmed that the crucial eyewitness evidence provided in 1945 by Tauber, Kula, and other survivors could be trusted. And it demonstrated that the blueprints, which the SS forgot to destroy in early 1945 when they abandoned the camp, and the remains of the gas chambers and crematoria, which they did blow up before their departure, could confirm that history if coaxed by forensic analysis.

The globally reported trial destroyed whatever credibility Holocaust deniers still enjoyed in the eyes of some significant sections of the general public. Irving was the deniers' champion and he failed miserably; truth triumphed over lies. And many Holocaust survivors, who had followed the trial proceedings with great anxiety, heaved a sigh of relief: in a more distant future, the historical record concerning the Holocaust would be safe in the hands of conscientious historians who base historical interpretation on the study of all the relevant facts and articulate facts based on the study of all the available evidence.

I published the Auschwitz evidence and the way it played out in the trial in *The Case for Auschwitz: Evidence from the Irving Trial* (2002)—a book that combines the genres of historical study and memoir. Five years after its publication, I gave Alejandro Aravena a copy when he visited the University of Waterloo School of Architecture. After reading it, he wrote to me that the book had made him feel like "a privileged witness to an issue that makes the man a man, and is told in first person (*en primera persona* as we say in Spanish)."[9] Another eight years later, after his appointment as Artistic Director of the 2016 Venice Architecture Biennale, Aravena invited me to present my work on the forensic, evidentiary significance of the Auschwitz gas chambers and crematoria as it had played in the trial, offering me the fifty-square-metre-large Room Q in the Central Pavilion, the former Padiglione Italia. He included an outline for the Biennale. Entitled *Reporting from the Front*, it began with a bold statement: "There are several battles that need to be won...." Yes, I thought, and although the court found for the defence and Irving was routed, the battle against Holocaust denial still continues. Motivated both by the honour of the invitation, the rightful place of the battle I had been involved in within a larger exposition on battles involving architecture, and the opportunity it offered, I accepted the invitation.

In the correspondence that contained the invitation, Aravena mentioned that he had been intrigued by the drama and the theatricality of my engagement as a witness in the courtroom—elements that I had described in some detail in *The Case for Auschwitz*. "Just thinking out loud, I thought of something like recreating a court where an attorney is standing and you decide to stand too, so that he has to look up. This is already an architectural operation that is worth being highlighted (and eventually reenacted with a dummy for example). And then go to the architectural proofs, like the way the door opens, where the steel bars are to protect the glass, and ultimately to the hole in the roof: how such an apparently harmless detail can dismantle a huge negationist movement."[10]

Aravena's idea evolved into the idea of creating an evidence room in which the drama was not to be located in the witness, but in the evidence (which is derived from the Latin verb *vidēre*, "to see") itself, in the visual concentration of evidence in all its apparent muteness. With important input from my wife, Miriam, a veteran in Holocaust education, my partners Donald, Anne, Sascha, and I, and the students who joined us, decided to apply Pevsner's judgment on Nazi architecture—"the less said the better"—to our exhibition. No videos, no reams of explanation, just the evidence itself. The centre of the room would be occupied by full-size reconstructions of three key pieces of evidence in the trial: a gas column from Crematorium 2, a gastight door with peephole in its frame, and a piece of the wall from Crematorium 5 with a gastight shutter and a ladder that allows an SS man carrying a tin of Zyklon-B to reach it. The periphery would offer casts of documents: blueprints, letters, and drawings by survivors.

As I write this at the end of February, the elements of *The Evidence Room*, which will come together in Venice, are filling our studio. The plaster exhibits fill the drying racks, the gas column is ready to be painted, and the boards of the door and shutter are joined. And I cannot but recall Dame Frances' description of Camillo's Memory Theatre, a temporary installation intended to be a "built or constructed mind and soul."[11] And I realize, with a shock of recognition, that for the few months that it existed, five centuries ago, it too stood in Venice.

1   Jean Cayrol, *Nuit et Brouillard* (Paris: Éditions mille et une nuits, 2010), 16; Jean Cayrol, "Night and Fog," in Robert Hughes ed., *Film: Book 2—Films of Peace and War* (New York: Grove Press, 1962), 236.

2   Nikolaus Pevsner, *An Outline of European Architecture, Jubilee Edition* (Harmondsworth: Penguin, 1960), 671.

3   As quoted in Frances Yates, *The Art of Memory* (London: Routledge & Kegan Paul, 1966), 132.

4   David Irving, "Battleship Auschwitz," *The Journal of Historical Review*, vol. 10 (1990), 498–9.

5   Fred A. Leuchter, *The Leuchter Report: The End of a Myth* (Decatur, Alabama: David Clark, n.d.), 7.

6   For my involvement in the case see Robert Jan van Pelt, *The Case for Auschwitz: Evidence from the Irving Trial* (Bloomington and Indianapolis: Indiana University Press, 2002).

7   Germar Rudolf, quoted in van Pelt, *The Case for Auschwitz*, 501.

8   Quoted in ibid., 464–5.

9   Message, Alejandro Aravena to Robert Jan van Pelt, January 4, 2008.

10  Message, Alejandro Aravena to Robert Jan van Pelt, July 28, 2015.

11  As quoted in Yates, *The Art of Memory*, 132.

Correspondence
– Donald McKay

Saturday, January 16, 2016
at 8:53 PM
From a hotel room in Venice

Dear Robert Jan,

On first riding the Blue Line boat into the city in the dark, dark, dark, I wondered (besides the obvious) what in the world I was doing here: Venice is so far from my nature. It isn't one of my cities—NYC, London, Paris, places for flâneurs of one sort or another—the cities that site themselves in the centre of my personal mythology. That feeling lasted until I stepped off the boat and walked past Harry's Bar... about 30 seconds after landing.

My room is virtuous and hot and right on a canal, facing into a little square on one side and onto the canal, across from the Bauer, on the other. I DO admire the subversive modernism of the Bauer. I'm sure [1] I want to stay there some time, and [2] I'll hate it. There are still tourists here, even now, in the cold, but they are all older, and *sans enfants* (mostly), and they make up an oddly native class, a class of people who seem to be the appreciative and necessary visitors to Venice, effectively its current audience, much like the middle-aged breakfast company I enjoyed in Paris on my last visit belonged there too. That is, in the funhouse, the clowns are welcome. And respectful. And VERY badly dressed.

Sascha and I meet tomorrow in front of the Bauer to go off and plan our campaign, but I know where it is I want to spend my afternoon—the Punta della Dogana, one of the two museums in Venice that belongs to the François Pinault Foundation. I want to feel the effect of the late 20th century on this city, where I think I have the best hope for a real framework to look back into it. And, since Corb never built the hospital, I will have to settle for Ando.

I'm almost perfectly prepared for Monday. The "paragraph" (I wrote to the University of Waterloo purchasing department) stole my last moments of preparation on Friday (so long ago!), and I didn't print out my pages of notes, but I'll transcribe all my concerns into a notebook and go with that, along with several reduced sets of the most current drawings, as if multiplying them makes them more real.

And as to our current state (with purchasing): I'm no longer apoplectic with fury about it, but I am SO exasperated. It's like a crisis in some Indiana Jones movie: beat off one terrible threat, and a greater, more vicious, even less vulnerable adversary springs up. Of course, that is any great heroic tale, so I'm glad the Venetians claim Hercules for their own; we need the ass-hat. I know you have a thousand responsibilities next week, but this one is worth a fortune to us: to be this close, seeing our way clear to the end, and have it snatched away.... It's unbearable. Indeed, if it needs the President's intervention, then do not hold back.

In spite of a tablet, two beers, and a bad night's sleep last night, I'm having a tough time sleeping now, but I suppose I should try again.

And I MISS my daughter here. For me, no one is better to be with in another city. (Via a long text exchange) I told her, after my first visit here, in I think 1978, I swore I wouldn't be coming back until I was invited. (I exempted the visit here a few years ago for New Year's with her and her mother.) Robin wrote back that she sensed a story. I dug up an explanation: this is a city where I'd rather be a small part of the show than a small part of the audience.

So, certainly, thirty-eight years later, let's be part of the show. Dammit!

Love to M,
Donald

*Written after a delayed nine-and-a-half-hour flight, departing close to midnight, from Toronto to Frankfurt, where I miss my connection and re-acquaint myself with good German salami and better beer, before catching a later flight to Venice, in order to find the Blue Line airport waterbus in the dark, and cruise the black water of the lagoon to the Lido, and finally to the dock by Harry's Bar, a hotel room, and a fine dinner.*

*My departure is marred by a ruling that comes down from the University of Waterloo purchasing department only an hour or so before the cab arrives. The conditions of the ruling would set back our plans for manufacture of key parts of the exhibition by four to six weeks. Happily, Robert Jan and the administrators in the School of Architecture smooth the waters by afternoon of the following Monday, and Sascha and I have a diplomatic and fruitful three days of meetings with Biennale staff in Venice. In the afternoons, after the meetings, I wander the city for a couple of hours before retreating to my room to write reports and revise drawings on my laptop. I try to nap before going to dinner, but the tiny square my room looks onto is a gondolier's station. They congregate in numbers until 7:00 in the evening, waiting for a passenger or two, talking loudly, telling bad jokes, laughing, and singing bawdy songs. No sleep is possible. At dinner Monday night, one Venetian guest argues that gondoliers are the WORST. I'm reminded of British football fans.*

*I return from Venice in a much better frame of mind, even if the Punta della Dogana is closed and will be until April, when I will return with a team and an exhibition.*

Tuesday, February 23, 2016
*The Evidence Room* Studio
Cambridge


This column COULD have been made this way. It's very likely. It
doesn't mean it WAS made this way. But it could have been.
– Bob Intini, spoken during a meeting at his stamping shop
in Hamilton


The first crisis, the crisis where I found myself asking what it was we
were doing and how it was we were doing it, came early in this enterprise, before there was a team—just Robert Jan, Anne, and myself
(we hadn't invited Sascha to join us yet). Before there was a team,
there were three volunteers: Michael and Tom Nugent, and Bob Intini.
When we had next to no money, they took my drawings and set out to
build a pair of gas columns—one for Venice and one for Montreal.
    I could call this the crisis of the rivets; but really, it was our first
crisis of intention. In the beginning, it was played out in emails; it
finally concluded in a meeting. A small crisis, but the first lesson.

Over the fall, with only enough money to plan *The Evidence Room*,
I work the way I usually do, at both ends: in notebooks, editing the
principals of the project for myself, and in the computer, preparing
drawings. The notebooks describe a strategy, the drawings describe
the tactics, beginning in close, with key details, and at a distance, by
organizing the overall order—describing the circumstances, the critical
dimensions, the centrelines of structural members, control lines of all
sorts—regulating the plan, the section, the space. Each mitigates the
other; they both go forward. What I am really doing is building the
project in my mind and editing it at the same time. And two of those
twenty-four sheets of drawings describe the gas column, the poisoning
machine that makes our first crisis.
    The entire project comes in four parts. First there are *the three
monuments*—full-scale building components, our replicas of the
architectural killing machine. Then there are *the exhibits*—plaster
casts of drawings, images, and components that put the monuments
in context. *The matrix* is the third part—the framework that makes
the two opposing walls that hold the exhibits. The fourth part is the
site, the room we are building the exhibition into—its dimensions, the
entrances, equipment that furnishes the space, the lighting, the rooms
on either side of it.
    In the first hour of the project, in our first conversation, perhaps
because I've been working with plaster casts for the last two years
and whiteness is everywhere for me, I know we will render the entire

exhibition in shades of white. Robert Jan has many good reasons for the universal whites, but for me, the white distances the monuments and the exhibits from the originals, making them evidence, rather than replicas.

The "white decision" helps us in the early weeks of the project, designing these things that are not designed. Finding the appropriate tone for any of these parts—especially the three monuments—is difficult. When I design, it's hard to acknowledge evil.

There are daily conversations about the exhibits, the plaster casts, but they are Anne's problem, Anne and her team, and, except as occasional kibitzer, I stay out of that conversation. When the team finishes with the casts, they will make the walls of the space and they will tell the story, for people patient enough to study them.

The matrix occurs to me first as a scaffold of pipes. The scaffold seemed neutral enough, like the armature for an archaeological fragment, but whenever I pictured scaffold of any sort, with its inevitable knuckle-ish connections, it seems too coarse, too intrusive, too present. In biology the matrix is that tissue between specialized cells; in mathematics the matrix is a rectangular array of numbers or symbols; in geology the matrix is a fine-grained material embedded with larger objects. And in printing the matrix is the mould in which letters are cast. The matrix is both present, as a medium, and absent, as a factor in itself. Pipe scaffolding has no natural depth, and we need depth as much as we need self-effacement.

Lying awake one night, while the project is in its infancy, before it is first drawn, I realize I have the device at hand. I adapt a system of bookcases I first designed and manufactured a decade earlier, furnishings fabricated from eighteen-gauge sheet steel, folded to make profiles two and three millimetres wide, leaving the matrix to represent nothing in the room but the lines of its own regulation. It is a near-perfect archaeological armature: quick to assemble, smooth, deferential, a servant to the exhibits and their infrastructure. Part of the matrix—the screened ceiling, fragile and boring—draws the exhibition together into a room, and rescues that room from some very insistent ceiling diffusers. We finish it in a custom-coloured powder coat, material left over with the completion of the new Whitney Museum. With "Whitney White," we make a small homage to Renzo Piano. For the matrix, it seems appropriate.

The three monuments, on the other hand, require a constant attention, calling up some sort of design theory that works to escape design. There are no easy, prefabricated solutions here.

Like everyone on the team who finally comes to the project, I work from photographs taken in the ruins of Auschwitz, and from dimensions of the few surviving fragments, to draw the gas hatch and the gas chamber door. The gas column is recorded in no more than a child's sketch, in accounts of survivors and guards, and, very thinly, in architectural drawings of the gas chambers. In life, the gas columns are gone, taken, the gas chambers dynamited. They are present in their absence, in the configurations of reinforcing in the concrete that has survived the explosives, leaving only evidence of the columns' passing. In my first drawings of the project, drafted on my screen in the last week of August and rendered in the computer over the Labour Day weekend by Nicole Ratajczak, I prepare drawings of the matrix, the gas chamber door, and the gas hatch, but it is Nicole who prepares the first iteration of the gas column, based on earlier sketches and interpretations drawn by or for Robert Jan. Perhaps I am more comfortable working with known quantities. With Nicole's effort, these drawings result in images that find their way to the first fundraising literature; they persist for weeks after.

In the intervening weeks, when the promises of early funding evaporate, Anne, Robert Jan, and I meet and reduce costs. A single astute observation on Anne's part simplifies the matrix. And a flu-enforced three-week period at home, at my desk, leaves me time to redraw the entire project, and work through the gas column for myself. Nicole's drawings, based on a few minutes' sketching between the two of us, contain a crucial error, and Robert Jan corrects it. And then I'm left to myself, face-to-face with the gas column.

I draw it a half-dozen times, each iteration stripping away finesse. This is the moment when I am "designing these things that are not designed." The art resides in an effort to be artless without being deliberately crude. It takes me only one iteration to eliminate every hex bolt in favour of square-head bolts. It takes me three iterations before I eliminate every mitred joint. It takes four before I have a sense of when to butt a connection and when to lap it. I search out the essence of these things, understanding, as I never have before, the essence of a thing might not always be edifying, but it could be enlightening. Each refinement leaves the column a little less refined; at each stage, the brute becomes more monumental. Perversely, this is satisfying. I wonder how much I am channeling the slave workers— the ironworkers or blacksmiths who probably built these things—and how much I am channeling the Nazi inventors. I love one, I loath the other; my hands work for both, in concert.

The story of Michael and Tom and Bob is told elsewhere, so I won't add much to it, except for the story of the first crisis. On November 20, when Robert Jan and I pick up Michael on a street corner in Toronto to drive to Hamilton where Michael and his father, Tom, introduce us to Bob Intini, I have a set of drawings of the gas

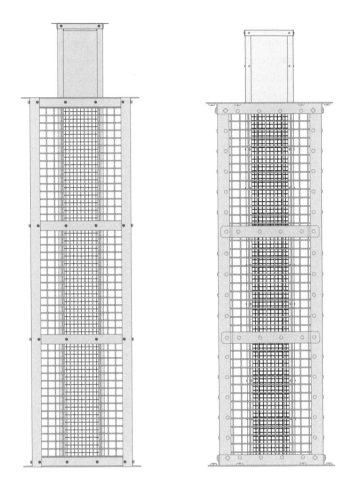

fig. 64                    fig. 65

column. I'm settled: I've found the appropriate balance between the idea and the effect. In Hamilton, we tour Bob's shop, where I am very happy, and we settle on steel profiles and wire screens and bolts. And, now that we have committed to the project on the ground, Robert Jan, Anne, and I invite Sascha to formally join us in a fresh campaign of funding, and I push the column to the back of my mind.

But all the while, there is a stream of news coming out of Hamilton: historically-appropriate woven wire mesh doesn't have the structural integrity of welded wire mesh; portions of the assembly need to be beefed up, but it won't show; strategies for prefabrication and disassembly change; the weight goes up. As the changes mount I email Michael to ask for shop drawings, the drawings a manufacturer prepares from the design drawings to coordinate conception and execution before building. Michael writes:

Everything is on track as we near completion, but the reality is I won't be able to do as-built drawings until, well, it's built. We need to assemble everything for me to get accurate dimensions of the entire piece and the drawings won't go together until that's done... Short version: trust us.
If there are details which you feel need to be changed we can do that after you see it.

Michael attaches a photograph of the outside of the two-part column. I'm alarmed. There are mitres where I show none, there are laps where I show butts, butts where I show laps. And there are rivets. Large rivets. Prominent rivets. I sense too much conscientious craft, and too much style. This is channeling the artisan, but not the despot. I worry, and resolve to get to Hamilton as soon as I can. As soon as I can comes two days before Christmas, the day after a funding event, when I'm confident we have the money to manufacture the rest of the show, even if we have to tip it into the lagoon after the Biennale, because there is still no money to bring it home again. The column has been in other people's hands for a month, and I am anxious to see what has become of it.

Intention, in this case, is not something that responds to a simple policy. I find myself thinking of a day in Paris that fall, with my daughter, after the first design of *The Evidence Room*, but before the second. I'm preoccupied with the book I'm writing, a book that passes through Paris in the Twenties, a book that looks at politics and sculpture and photography. My daughter and I have these occasional days of flâneury, when we savour a great city in some particular way, on foot. That day, we are going to spend some hours with the *Nike of*

*Samothrace* at the Louvre, before we go to wander the Père Lachaise Cemetery for the afternoon.

The epitome of frozen motion, the *Nike* fascinates me, as it has so many people for twenty-five centuries. Recently, the curators at the Louvre restored the statue, not for the first time. The restoration makes the *Nike* a tourist attraction, and a rolling crowd of as many as a hundred people press on the vast stair landing where it stands. Most of these people don't look at the statue; instead the selfie-stick rules, so they look away from the *Nike of Samothrace* and into the screens where they see themselves pose with the statue in the background; it becomes the setting for their travels, and their travels are a commodity, attested to in dozens of self-portraits. After an hour of this frustration, my daughter signals, "Enough!" and we move on, to the next room, the room that has been the restoration workshop. Unattended, empty, this is the space the curators have chosen, where they tell the story of that restoration. Taken down from the stone boat's prow that is its base, taken to this room nearby, conservators work on the statue for as much as a year. They clean and repair, but they do not undo the work of previous restorations. As much as a quarter of the statue we know in photographs is plaster. The restorers choose to clean and preserve the plaster, rather than remove it. Much of the torso, with its veil of wet, wind-whipped fabric, is a modern interpolation, an interpretation of the ancient statue. This construction remains part of the *Nike* now. The cultural memory of the statue, and its effect, trump historic purity.

So, I arrive in Hamilton in a state of confusion, bound to respect the artisanal sensibility that has re-rendered my column, intent on ensuring that the final effect is neither too crafted, nor too styled. The mitres vanish in the opening negotiations and I cede the laps where I first saw butt connections. But the rivets are a problem. Bob refers to vintage manuals, we draw back and forth, we study alternatives, I try to describe the effect, we speculate on the role of the white paint. Finally, we discuss a compromise: Bob leaves the room with a sample of angle and the offending rivet, and returns twenty minutes later with the material still hot and the rivet milled down and much reduced. I'm satisfied, and the volunteers will spend two days milling down eight hundred more rivets. A month later Tom tells me it took Bob three minutes to reduce the rivet that day, that he stayed out of the room for dramatic effect and, for the same reason, torch-heated the sample just before he returned. As much as I do, Bob understands artifice.

While we are negotiating the details in the office of his shop, Bob— tapping the sample of a riveted connection—makes the best point:

"This column COULD have been made this way. It's very likely. It doesn't mean it WAS made this way. But it could have been."

That's my mantra just now, in the midst of making all these things. As Anna Longrigg and Siobhan Allman draw versions of doors and hatches, as Tom Nugent and Bradley Paddock wrestle with ancient wood salvaged from barns and iron forged in other shops, I return to that mantra. We are acrobats, dancing on a line between truth and effect, and we strive every day to be honest as we tell the story.

And in the midst of making all these things, Venice comes closer.

To Build a Gas Column
– Michael Nugent

*At the time I didn't know it, but my involvement in this project had begun two-and-a-half years earlier, on a sunny afternoon in early September. We sat crowded in a lecture hall at the University of Waterloo School of Architecture. Seventy-seven first-year students, excited, laughing, anticipating our journey into the world of architecture. We were children then, fresh-faced and naïve, like the generations of students before us, living in the illusions of a world we didn't understand.*

The children who entered that room were not the ones who left. Part of them had been taken by another room, from another time, in another place: a room that stole the lives of more children, grandparents, mothers, fathers, brothers, sisters, friends, and lovers than any other place on earth. Two thousand people, in a two-hundred-square-metre room, every day, for two-and-a-half years. Professor Robert Jan van Pelt had given us our first lecture on the history of architecture—specifically, the architecture of Auschwitz. He took us through the drawings, showed us details designed for the mass murder of human beings: the direction of door swings, the placement of handles. Stairs going in. Slides going out. At the end he asked us to make a promise, a promise never to use the skills we would learn to design for genocide. To never build the tools for another Holocaust.

Two years later, on a similarly sunny afternoon in early September, Robert Jan came to me with a request. He had been invited to create an exhibition of architectural and mechanical evidence from Auschwitz at the Venice Biennale; he and our colleague Donald McKay were putting together key artifacts and they wanted my help as a fabricator.

For two months I heard nothing from either of them until I knocked on Robert Jan's office door in November. Robert Jan looked up from his desk, tired and worried. "Oh, thank God, Michael Nugent. I need a hug. I'm so fucked." He told me they weren't getting the support— financial or otherwise—that they needed. Consequently he and Donald had been forced to drastically condense the exhibition and the project was in peril. But they understood that the key to saving it—and to producing an incredibly powerful Holocaust exhibition—was the only piece of evidence never recovered: the gas columns used to lower Zyklon-B into the gas chambers. He asked me, and my father, to recreate one for Venice.

My father, Tom Nugent, is a mechanical engineer and craftsman who spent his career in manufacturing and industrial system design. I had worked with him from a young age and was now versed in many of the same fields, in addition to time I had spent working for a blacksmith and fabricator. Together, we had the rudimentary knowledge to build the gas column.

Nonetheless, we knew that we would need a third man. Bob Intini, my father's best friend, is a prolific tool-and-die maker, operating one of the last stamping shops in Hamilton. He is also deeply knowledgeable as a machine, train, and automobile historian. His thorough insight into period fabrication methods would be invaluable in this endeavour. When I asked them for help, there was no hesitation. We understood that this needed to be done. That night, we told Robert Jan and Donald we were in.

The following week, Donald, Robert Jan, and I travelled to Hamilton to meet with my father and Bob. The five of us discussed the project, the preliminary details of construction, material weight, and site assembly. But the key issue remained: there was no formal historical documentation of the columns. Only a handful of eyewitness accounts from survivors and camp staff, along with a fifteen-year-old boy's drawing, done shortly after his liberation.

It was clear that this was not something elegant, refined at a drafting table. It was a brute, crudely sketched out by a member of the SS and built in the camp workshops by men whose names had been stolen and replaced by numbers. It was left to us to recreate it, to build something monstrous that could withstand the force of two thousand people, pressed together, panicking, ten people per square metre, fighting to live. Dying. Day after day. Understanding this, we began fabrication of the column on November 20, 2015.

Fabrication is a difficult thing. Despite the noise of machinery and showers of sparks, it is conducted in complete silence. Words are lost over the machinery, voices are muffled out by ear defenders. Actions are repetitive, tedious. You withdraw from the task, left with your thoughts—thoughts of what you're doing, what you're making, as the hideous thing comes together in your hands. Lunch breaks are spent laughing and telling stories, a reprieve from the task at hand. Robert Jan says the Holocaust produces a very black sense of humour. When faced with recreating this *thing*, how can you not wrap yourself in the armour of laughter?

But after a while it gets to you anyway, creeping through the cracks in your armour. You stop, put down your tools. Walk away.

Every time I weld, my mask goes black. Every time it goes black, I see the lights go out, hear the screams of innocent lives being snuffed out. Bodies twisted and mangled, children trampled to death, unrecognizable piles of corpses smashed into the corners of the room. Yet the space around the columns is left completely bare, a last effort to escape the gas.

And there is a lot of welding.

So you dehumanize yourself. It stops being a gas column; it becomes just a pile of steel that needs to be worked. Otherwise, it would

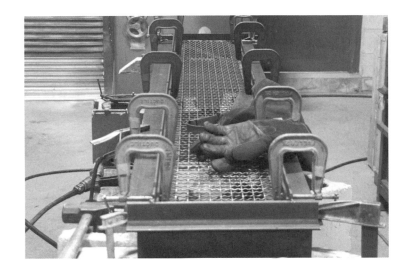

fig. 66

completely consume you. You think about how nice it is to spend time with your mentors, about how much you enjoy metalwork, about that episode of television the night before, about the girl you like, about what it's going to be like seeing it in Venice. You think about everything but what it is. Ten hours a day, three days a week for two months.

One of Bob's colleagues who grew up on a farm comes by one day, puts his fingers through the quarter-inch-thick wire cage we are using for the outer panels and gives it a good shake. "Pigs get through that in six months. Can't imagine what people would do." It takes a while to shake that one off.

Then one day I look down at the pile of steel I am working and, for the first time, I truly understand what it is. I can no longer distance myself from what I am doing. Because that's how genocide happens: you dehumanize yourself, you dehumanize them. You give them a different name—Jews, Swine, Menace, something, anything besides what they are: human beings. Each one with his or her own history, struggles, beliefs, loves. From that day on, I go to work understanding the full gravity of what I am doing.

We build the column as an assembly of components—standard, symmetrical, interchangeable, inert. Sets of two, four, eight, and sixteen. It makes it easier to work. The first time we assemble the pieces it is little more than the outer frame and two cage panels. It stands there, not a column in a room, but a freestanding, cruel black tower. We gather around it, Bob, my father, and me. We smile with pride at all the hard work that has gone into it thus far. Then something creeps into my head as I step back: "I heard a voice in the midst of the four beasts, and I looked and behold: a pale horse. And his name, that sat on him, was Death. And Hell followed with him." My smile twists with disgust, my stomach drops, and the taste of ash fills my mouth.

I have broken the promise we had made to Robert Jan more than two years ago.

From that moment on the column had form and it left its mark on anyone who saw it: shop visitors, customers, deliverymen, and family members. Each one of them curious, each one reacting differently: shock, anger, disgust, gratitude. Sadness. I saw grown men brought to tears simply at the sight of it, leaving before they lost all control. I saw a child look up to his grandfather, asking what it was, tugging at his sleeve while his grandfather stood stoically, jaw clenched, fighting back tears. I am glad that I was not in the car for the conversation after.

And then my time working on it ended. I returned to school. I tried to push it out of my mind but I couldn't. I couldn't escape my thoughts of the people who had been changed by the gas column. It left its mark on them. It has left its mark on me.

Six weeks later I saw it finished, naked, before it would be covered by a veil of white paint. It stood there in front of me, menacing, hideous, sublime. I couldn't help but gravitate to it, but the primal animal inside me smelled death and said, "Run. Run and don't stop until you're far from this thing." And I felt incredibly small in its presence.

Small in the world.

Generations
– Tom Nugent

In late November 2015, Donald, Robert Jan, and Michael drove to Hamilton to meet with Bob Intini and myself. Michael had already told the story of the project and asked Bob if he could use his facility to do some fabrication. After a brief introduction, Robert Jan dove into the essence of *The Evidence Room*, presenting the history of the Holocaust and the mechanics of death. Donald rolled out a CAD drawing of the gas column and then started sketching a simplified version of it in a Moleskine notebook. Looking across the table I saw him write "2400 mm." That one dimension gave me the height of the overall column and was all I really needed. On our way to the steel store around the corner, I committed to the project. Time and money were not an issue. Michael's enthusiasm, the moving narrative from Robert Jan and Donald—these were all that Bob and I needed.

A marathon later, we had the columns built. Then, at the beginning of January, Donald phoned me at home to ask if I would join the team as an advisor. This was old school—just picking up the phone, no need to forward or reply all—but I wanted Michael's approval before I agreed.

The next day, I met with the team in Donald's office. After a round table introduction, Donald rolled out the project scope, the timeline, and the budget. No one individual in the room could accomplish this. I had a sinking feeling—there was not enough time or money and the team was green. If things went south, what I valued most—my relationship with my son—would be hurt. But I realized that three professors and a producer were entrusting their reputations to a select group of students, so I trusted too.

And over the next few weeks, I was amazed. The team came alive. They were playing to win. This was not a corporate defensive game with political agendas. Each person was working to his or her full potential: collaborating, experimenting with ideas, and working in a positive environment.

With the development, the money came in. The principals—Donald, Robert Jan, Anne, and Sascha—handed over much of the responsibility to the student team. They no longer worried about them; they only had to care about them. It was a pleasure to come into the school every Tuesday for the roundtable sessions. Things were happening. Not just good things, but great things. *The Evidence Room* was happening. The 2016 Venice Biennale was happening.

In the end, teamwork, openness, brutally frank discussion, project management, and trust have made this project. I have gained a lot: understanding how to tell a story in an exhibition format, meeting the visitors to the project, and interacting with the team. I can see how the Waterloo School of Architecture shapes a generation.

*Tagebuch einer Halbdeutsche*
– Sascha Hastings

## 1979

Grade 5. I'm walking home from school with friends. Somehow Germany comes up. A boy I have a crush on snarls the word "Germany" and spits on the sidewalk. My ten-year-old heart is shattered. How can he hate a whole country? Does this mean he hates my mother? Does he hate me too?

## 1980

I see my first images of the Holocaust in a film shown by my teacher. The sunken cheeks and hollowed-out eyes staring from the bunks. The emaciated bodies stacked like cords of wood. I knew the Germans had started the war. I knew they were the bad guys. I didn't know they had done this.

## 1988

I spend the summer in Munich as an intern at the German Theatre Museum. On weekends I go on short trips—even as far as Venice. Dachau is at the end of the S2 commuter train line and easy to get to. For some reason I never make it there.

## 1989

I come home late from class on the night of November 9. My parents are watching the news. People are drinking, crying, dancing, and embracing on the Berlin Wall, while others clamber up to join them. The wall has fallen.

The next morning the newspaper has a photograph of people on the wall in front of the Brandenburg Gate. "Oh my God," I say, "That's Peter!" Unbelievably, a friend of mine is among them. I tell my parents I have to go to Berlin. Now. They freak out—they remember Hungary and the Prague Spring. To my eternal regret, I allow myself to be infected by their fear. So instead, I book a flight to Munich to stay with my cousins.

In Munich, there is very little evidence of what has just happened, with the exception of the occasional Trabi car that putters through the city. West Germans wave or honk at the "Ossis" [East Germans] in the Trabi and they grin, wave, and honk back. Mostly my cousins and I are glued to the TV, where there is non-stop coverage of the events unfolding in Berlin, events that I follow from a safe distance.

I am in Germany with my parents to see my grandmother, who is in hospital. We take a long weekend to go to Weimar. While there we also visit Buchenwald. There isn't much to see. A desolate field where the barracks once stood, bitterly cold even in July. We see the room where people were shot in the back of the head and the ovens in the crematorium. There is a museum. My mother doesn't want to go in. My dad and I stay outside with her.

## 1992

I am a graduate student at the University of Freiburg in Germany, where I have developed a nice circle of friends. But almost all of them have terrible relationships with at least one parent, to the point of not speaking. Their parents have terrible relationships with their parents too. I wonder how things got so fucked up. I think how lucky I am that the war and the Holocaust haven't affected me.

## 1995

I am at the cottage with my parents. A German farmer and his wife, from whom we have bought vegetables for years, come for tea. Everything is fine until he starts talking about "the Jews." It gradually becomes clear that his "holidays" in Germany are trips to disseminate antisemitic propaganda. Being Canadian, we are too polite, or conflict-averse, to throw them out, so we say as little as possible and just wait for them to leave.

## 1999

I am in Berlin with a colleague, producing a CBC radio series on the arts ten years after the fall of the Berlin Wall. We walk through Schöneberg, where artists have installed a memorial made up of double-sided signs mounted on lampposts around the neighbour-hood. One side has the text of one of the many anti-Jewish laws passed between 1933 and 1945 and the other a corresponding image. As we walk through the streets we experience the sick but brilliant strategy of the racial laws: if you take away people's rights little by little, nobody will object; by the time the cumulative effect is clear it's too late.

My colleague is Jewish. I ask what it's like for her to be in Berlin. She says fine, except occasionally she gets an irrational fear: "What if they come to get me?" She knows I'm half German. I wonder how she feels about this, but I don't ask.

## 2002

I produce a radio piece with the artists involved in Canada's exhibition at the Venice Architecture Biennale. It's the first time I've heard of the Biennale. One of them invites me to come with them to Venice. I am desperately tempted but have already booked a trip to Berlin and can't do both. "One day," I tell myself, "I will work on the Biennale."

## 2007

I am at Robert Jan van Pelt's place for dinner. I'm deep in conversation with his partner, Miriam. I tell her that I'm half German but that I probably have some Jewish ancestors somewhere. She looks at me and says, "All Germans say that."

## 2009

I have just spent two weeks in Rome, followed by a week in Venice. It's my first time in Rome and the first time I've been back to Venice since I was eighteen. I am blown away. I have completely lost interest in Germany. Wow. I didn't see this coming at all.

Later that year, I am invited to work on the Canada Pavilion at the 2010 Venice Architecture Biennale. I can't believe my luck.

## August 2015

I am in Rome taking Italian lessons. Everyone tells me that I speak Italian with a German accent. I'm proud that nobody takes me for an American, but a bit uncomfortable about being pegged as German.

Robert Jan contacts me to say he's been invited to exhibit at the 2016 Biennale. We talk at length about the project and, on his advice, I watch a NOVA documentary on the Irving trial. I had always assumed that the gas was pumped into the gas chambers through vents, but I discover that it was delivered through gas columns: the SS men opened a tin, tossed the Zyklon-B pellets into a basket, and lowered it down the column through a hole in the roof. The physical gesture reminds me of feeding fish in a tank or animals at the zoo, and shakes me to the core.

## December 2015

I am at a fundraising event for *The Evidence Room*. Robert Jan and Donald McKay speak eloquently about the project. I learn details that I didn't know before—how the space around the gas columns was always empty when the bodies were removed from the gas chamber; how there was no handle on the inside of the door; how the morgue was modified to become a gas chamber by replacing the body slide with steps (corpses don't walk). I nearly lose it.

## Mid-January 2016

I am in Venice with Donald to do site visits, meet with Biennale staff, and prepare for the installation. This is my fourth Biennale and I've loved them all, but I've never felt so strongly about any previous exhibition.

By coincidence, I have dinner with a friend of friends who turns out to be in charge of organizing the 500th anniversary of the Venice ghetto, the first ghetto ever, the one from which the term "ghetto" originated. That night I read up on its history and learn that in the sixteenth century, Venetian Jews had to wear a yellow circle or scarf whenever they left the ghetto. It appears that all roads lead to Venice... and to Auschwitz.

## Late January 2016

I am supposed to write a short piece for this book. But I'm not sure if what's going on inside me has any place here. I realize that working on *The Evidence Room* is in part a form of penance. And trying to do penance for the Holocaust is a German cliché. As is being crazy about Italy. Does penance in Venice really count as penance? Or is it just a very refined form of avoidance?

## February 2016

I think of the scene in *The Merchant of Venice* in which the Prince of Morocco has to choose one of three caskets in order to win Portia's hand. The caskets are made of gold, silver, and lead, but only one casket has her portrait in it. If he chooses the right one, he gets the girl. If not, he dies old and alone. The inscription on the gold casket reads, "Who chooseth me shall gain what many men desire." The one on the silver casket reads, "Who chooseth me shall get as much as he deserves." And the one on the lead casket reads, "Who chooseth me must give and hazard all he hath." Naturally, the Prince picks the gold casket, but inside he finds a skull with a scroll in its empty eye socket that begins with the words, "All that glisters is not gold."

Is *The Evidence Room* the lead chest? For Venice, and for each of us?

I write this piece. And I know I have to go to Auschwitz.

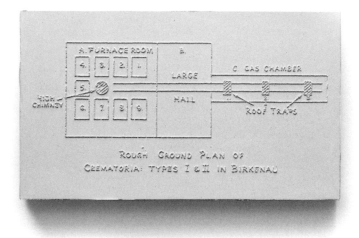

fig. 67

*The Evidence Room* points to different ideas—institutional, cultural, and architectural—of a room. *The Evidence Room* effectively rests on at least two contexts and their respective rooms—Courtroom 73 in the Royal Courts of Justice in London, where a libel trial was held in 2000, and Room Q of the Central Pavilion of the Venice Biennale where the exhibition *Reporting from the Front* is taking place in 2016. And obviously there are more rooms: the gas chambers at Auschwitz, the rooms of the Auschwitz-Birkenau State Museum today, and the Octagonal Room at the Canadian Centre for Architecture (Montreal) where elements of *The Evidence Room* will also be displayed.

The exhibition of the evidence in architectural venues brings additional histories to bear on the case for Auschwitz: in Venice, this evidence enters the history of the Biennale, the history of architecture, the history of architectural exhibitions, the contemporary display of architecture, the contemporary language of architecture, the contemporary concerns of architecture, etc. Our case, the case made by the evidence presented in Room Q, is deeply concerned with many of these contexts in which the issue of our relationship to history looms large.

The approach to the selection, the creation, and the display of the casts (what we also refer to as "the exhibits") is everywhere marked by the awareness of not just the necessity to bring forth the evidence for Auschwitz—which humanity must forever continue to do—but also by questions regarding the means by which the significance of history may be either affirmed or contested. Between the court and what are essentially exhibition venues, if not strictly speaking museums, how are the facts of history and life presented? By whom? Who has authority, and what does this authority entail? Who are the witnesses of the evidence presented at the Venice Biennale, and who constitutes the court? What is truthful, and how might we determine it? If understanding of the historical truth depends on the facts we may uncover and ascertain, our certainty ultimately relies upon our willingness to engage and be engaged by what is presented before us. Indeed, this readiness may be one of the few, if inadequate, bridges across "what happened" and what we can piece together, between the past in its actuality and how we account for it now.

In this respect, *The Evidence Room* is not only about the trial— about "revisiting" history or even about "authority" (the witness's, the court's, the expert's)—it is more generally about the necessity to remember what is undeniable and yet stands beyond comprehension. To remember what many would rather forget, if not deny. For this, scientific proofs and architectural forensics—and, of course, rhetoric—can be necessary in a courtroom to convince twelve jurors or a judge bound by the letter of the law, but not to the same extent for the human heart and the "cause" of memory. Unmediated by rhetoric, the casts in *The*

*Evidence Room* simply stand, as Dachau camp survivor Elly Gotz expressed to us in a February visit, as material witnesses that grant us the possibility to *feel* what we think and yet could never quite fathom: the unbearable reality of some of the darkest hours of our history.

The false debate around the holes in the roofs of Crematoria 2 and 3, holes through which Zyklon B pellets were lowered into the gas chambers below ground, provides one of the most powerful examples of these different ways of approaching truth. The question of the absence of these holes today has been raised many times since Auschwitz, even leading some to challenge the reality of the Holocaust. Responding to the absurd necessity to "prove" the existence of a void, Robert Jan van Pelt's architectural forensic work brought to light evidence that framed this void: sketches, descriptions, reinforcing bars in a collapsed roof, small dots on an aerial photograph. But calling for personal engagement in Room Q, it is through casting that we seek to convey the reality of history and this gap in humanity.

The plaster casts point to the inseparable complicity of what is present and absent, to lives lived and lives lost. Casting always carries the trace of another physical presence, that of the mould against which it was formed. As such, casts are undeniably tied to the physical reality. They are testimonies of existing evidence. Conversely, casts represent the materialization of the voids created by the moulds: they fill the negative space outlined by the mould. These moulds, in turn, are created through processes of translations—in time, in space, and through different media including tangible objects, drawings, letters, photographic reproductions, analogue and digital copies, and copies of copies. As a play between the constructed moulds and the possibility to recall what is absent, the casts question the reality of the material evidence. And while the fact that casts convey a sense of truthful representation by virtue of this physical relationship was important to our team as historians, the impact of their presence in the room was equally important to us as architects. Indeed, we settled on plaster casts because of the ghostly whiteness of plaster. In our "casts court," the casts operate between the scientific and the empathic, between the material evidence and its actual experience.

Symbolically and theoretically, the gravity of the topic called for casting in plaster. Practically though, there is very little that makes sense about casting in this specific context. How should one cast a letter written or typed in ink on a piece of A4 paper? How should we cast the blueprints, the photographs, the bills, or the drawings? Perhaps we should have simply cast them as blanks, and this might have shown the fragility of historical evidence. But we did not want to record the erasure of evidence but rather the potential for it to remain for those willing to look, and that decision implied that we had to build depth into drawings, letters, and photographs.

Significantly, the histories of drawing, of writing, and of photography all intersect with some dimensions of casting, and they are all deeply bound to the interplay between remembering and forgetting. For example, there is a direct link between the tools used for the creation of repetitive patterns in ceramic vessels and tiles to those used for the first printing presses.[1] This encounter between casting and printing is also prefigured in the use of the stylus and wax tablet in Antiquity. Wax, marked or written upon, was a common metaphor for memory. In his essay on memory and recollection, Aristotle likens an image held in memory in the soul, a "sort of imprint" in the mind, to the signet rings used to seal letters.[2] Cicero, in his *De oratore*, offers another well-known reference to this metaphor. Recounting Simonides' uses of the art of memory, he compares the mind's faculty of memory to the wax writing-tablet, wherein "the mental images of the things" one wishes to remember are like the letters written on it.[3]

Casting images in one's memory, facts on paper, or letters in plaster: all these processes point to a desire to record, to create a lasting trace, to remember. But none of these records are of any use without the ability and willingness to read them. We can evoke here Plato's recounting of the gift of writing to Thamus: rather than receiving the gift as a remedy to forgetting, as it was presented, Thamus warned that it only gave the *illusion* of remembering.[4] The distinction he was making was between appearance and engagement: for having something written, one will think that they know it, while in fact they will only *appear* to know it. Along the same lines, the historian Mary Carruthers reminds us that in Ancient Greece, there was no verb that actually meant "to read." The verb they used to designate the action of reading was *anagignosko*, which meant "to know again" or "to recollect." In Latin, she adds, the verb used for "to read" was *legere*, which literally translates as "to collect" or "to gather." In both cases, the terms refer to a mnemonic process, "the re-collection of 'gathered' material."[5]

Keeping these convoluted relationships between writing, reading, remembering, and forgetting, the casts of letters confront us with one fundamental aspect of casting as something to "read" in the Greek and Latin sense of the term: to approach as the "re-collection of gathered material." As casting necessarily implies a "having been," the casts of the letters confront us not only with their written content, but force us to engage with the past to which the present casts bear witness.

The idea of casting drawings brings up another set of considerations. The first drawing we tackled was the blueprint of Crematorium 2, drawn in October 1941. Originally, our intention was to maintain, as much as possible, the quality of the different types of evidence we were casting. For the drawing, this implied conveying the feeling of paper. Our first instinct was to turn to cardboard and make a simple outline of the plan. We did very little to the cardboard, accepting its presence as a kind of sacrificial mould—one that would get destroyed in the process of casting and only ever give one single plaster cast. The result, as imperfect and brittle as it was, was arresting. The texture of the cast—the presence of the lines, their shadows—seemed to both point to the immemorial origins of drawing as a tracing of the shadow, or *ichnographia*.

As is well known amongst architects, the term *ichnographia* was used by Vitruvius to refer to what is most commonly translated today as the architectural plan: the representation of what lies below a horizontal cut taken at a determined height. The simple translation of *ichnographia* to our contemporary conception of the "plan" does not encompass the full depth of the concept. Etymologically, *ichnographia* contains the root *graphia*, which is to draw, and *ichno*, which refers to notions of traces generally, and in some cases, to the marks left by the sun as it is cast against objects, in other words, shadows. These shadows everywhere permeate our approach to the drawings left by the architects of Auschwitz.

For architects, plans can be intimately linked to the rituals that take place in the buildings they draw. This idea meets its most frightful expression in the plans we were casting. Tracking the reversal of a door swing through a set of modifications, the standardization of gastight doors or gastight hatches in measurements repeated across sets of drawings, or the machine-like impression left by the ventilation of an underground gas chamber or of an incinerating system, the plaster casts of the blueprints left behind by the architects of Auschwitz offer the darkest shades of white and light. We were somewhat trapped by the strange urge to offer the crispest and most legible drawings, upset when part of a wall got caught in a mould, or when the dimensions of a gas-tight door were not as clear as we thought they ought to be. But ultimately, it is simply this relation between light and trace that needs to be communicated, and perhaps its potency lies precisely in its abstraction. After trying different heights for the walls or considering even leaving some colour residues from the cutting, we were content with the subtlest difference and the fact that a reading of a drawing could easily flip—that is, disappear or reappear—depending on the light source.

While at the beginning of the project we had the intention of using cardboard, wood, plaster, silicon, or acrylic moulds depending on the different evidence we were working against, we ended up with two main materials for the mould. For the small letters and bills, we settled for a soft basswood. For everything else, we used acrylic, but we used it differently for different types of evidence. Between texture, reflexivity, pixilation, striations, hatches, reliefs, engravings, matte or shiny finishes, the play between light and darkness can take many different modes. We systematically dealt with any typed or handwritten notes: casting raised letters. We took a rational approach to the drawings: raised walls, etched measurements, shiny background, and matte elevations. We adopted more nuances with the translation of the photographs, establishing four different depths that play off one another. Finally, we tried to reduce the sketches to their essence, using harsh black lines for graphite drawings or rough plaster surface for a messy sketch.

We henceforth became less concerned with the base material and more with the necessary abstraction that our process of casting implied. We have to remember that our casts are effectively the product of a number of translations involving, for example, a 1990s photograph of a 1942 blueprint, scanned, and cleaned digitally as well as with a stylus, so that it could be sent to the laser cutter, engraved in the acrylic, which was then prepared and sealed, before the plaster could finally be cast into it. But this abstraction also meant that we were creating new art works and, to a certain extent, flirting with aesthetics. We were trying to make good plaster casts. As frightening as it is, this must be acknowledged as it can hardly be avoided. We were engaged in conversations that involved symbolic and pragmatic questions that ranged from the legibility and subtlety of the images to the quality of the surface and the most desirable source of light. We were aware that the casts themselves harked back to other forms (the evidence, but also archaeological casts or specimens in a museum). We accepted how they pointed to their own making, but also welcomed how they could henceforth register further movement (one of us chipping a corner, dust accumulating, visitors touching them). We all intervened in the process, working diligently on every single piece of evidence: translating it; cutting and preparing the mould; mixing, casting, and curing the plaster; yet knowing—that is, remembering—that the work was not about any single one of these pieces.

Our trial and error process involved many decisions variously based on historical accuracy, efficiency, effect, or practicality. As we tested different approaches, the process of casting offered a constant reminder of the necessity to relinquish total control. In all the variables—the temperature of the water, the atmospheric conditions outside or in the room, the age of the plaster, the dust on the mould, the air in the mix, an unnoticed gap between the frame, or something else that we can never identify—there is always something in casting that is left as an unknown. Notwithstanding the projected outcome and the level of control maintained at every step of the process, the casts seem to have a life of their own. What will happen when you take off the mould, peel back the cardboard or the acrylic? Will the plaster have filled all the cavities?

Will the mix be sturdy enough? Will the surface have picked up the texture of the moulding material? What is the promise of the cast? The casts are evasive. In this respect, casting is not unlike history.

In the end, we have more than sixty plaster casts, separated in four bays, each loosely addressing one dimension of the forensic study. A first bay shows the larger region of Auschwitz and zooms in on the evidence of the missing holes. A second bay continues to track the transformations of the basements of Crematoria 2 and 3 and, more specifically, the change in the direction of the hinges of the door that originally opened into the gas chamber. A third bay focuses on Crematoria 4 and 5 and the orders and dimensions of the gastight doors and hatches. A final bay evidences the frightening burning capacity of the crematoria, with combustion and degassing accelerated by motors specially ordered for these purposes. The selection of the evidence and the way in which it is arranged, even though it is loosely related to a narrative, still defies comprehension. Like the process from which they were created, the story the casts tell cannot be fully comprehended and certainly never fully elucidated. The casts form the court of a history we inescapably share, courting the present to delve into its incomprehensible reality.

Hence, the "casts court," as we might call it, pleads silently, statically, and solemnly. It presents history as a site that is as contested as many contemporary situations. It displays drawings, constructions, and artifacts as intentional productions, indexes pointing to the hands that made them. It strips architecture of its mundane veil and reveals it in its bleakest light.

The room asks for a pause, questioning our relation to time and history as much as it questions the crowds rushing to see what is on at the Biennale this year. It offers a significant gap in time that for a split second might disrupt our obsession with the now and the future. It does not explain, nor elucidate. It merely poses a question that comes to its fullest answer when one effectively experiences the casts in their mute, fragile, ghostly, and yet indubitable presence.

1   See Cyril Stanley Smith, "Art, Technology, and Science," *Technology and Culture*, vol. 11, no. 4 (October 1970), 493–549, 513.

2   Aristotle, *De Memoria et Reminiscentia*, ed. and trans. Richard Sorabji, *Aristotle on Memory* (London: Duckworth, 1972), 450a25, 450b11.

3   Frances Yates, *The Art of Memory* (Chicago: University of Chicago Press and London: Routledge & Kegan Paul, 1966), 2.

4   Platon, *Phèdre*, trans. Luc Brisson (Paris: GF Flammarion, 1989), 178.

5   Mary Carruthers, *The Book of Memory: A Study of Memory in Medieval Culture* (Cambridge: Cambridge University Press, 1990), 30.

fig. 68

fig. 69                                          fig. 70 →

← fig. 71                    fig. 72

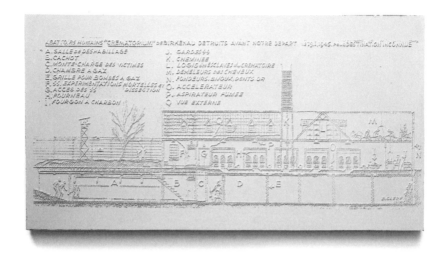

ABATTOIRS HUMAINS "CREMATORIUM," DE BIRKENAU DÉTRUITS AVANT NOTRE DÉPART 1941-1945. PAR DESTINATION INCONNUE

A . SALLE DE DESHABILLAGE
B . CACHOT
C . MONTE-CHARGE DES VICTIMES
D . CHAMBRE A GAZ
E . GRILLE POUR BOMBES A GAZ
F . SS. EXPERIMENTATIONS MORTELLES et DISSECTION
G . ACCES DES SS
H . FOURNEAU
I . FOURGON A CHARBON

J . GARDES SS
K . CHEMINEE
L . LOGIS DES ESCLAVES du CREMATOIRE
M . DEMELEURS des CHEVEUX
N . FONDEURS. BIJOUX, DENTS OR
O . ACCELERATEUR
P . ASPIRATEUR FUMEE
Q . VUE EXTERNE

fig. 73                              fig. 74 →

ABATTOIRS HUMAINS "CREMATORIUM"

A. SALLE DE DÉSHABILLAGE
B. CACHOT
C. MONTE-CHARGE DES VICTIMES
D. CHAMBRE A GAZ
E. GRILLE POUR BOMBES A GAZ
F. SS. EXPERIMENTATIONS MORTELLE
G. ACCES DES SS          DISSECTI
H. FOURNEAU
I. FOURGON A CHARBON

Lichte Höhe 200

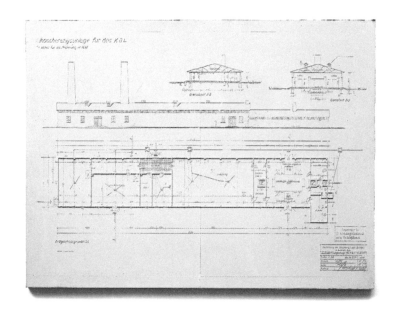

← fig. 75                                fig. 76

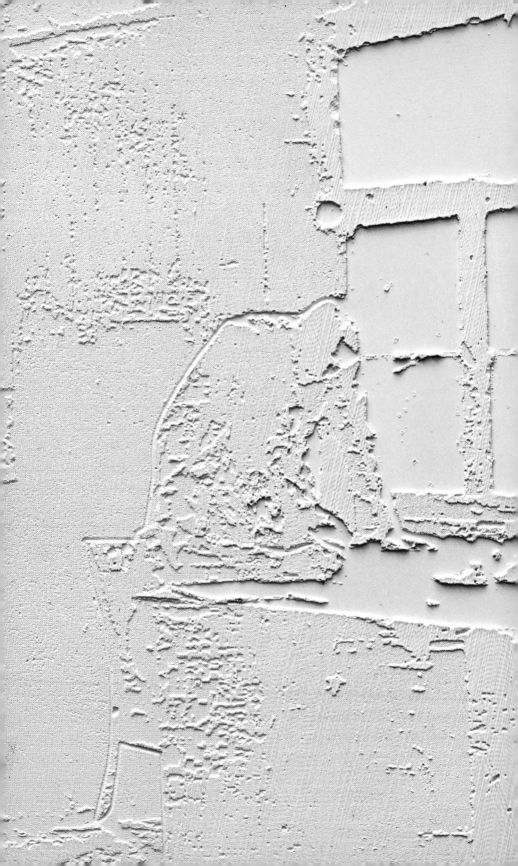

← fig. 79                              fig. 80

fig. 81

Buried in the forest, the grid plan of Auschwitz is a stark piece of evidence of the architecture systematically and purposefully built for death—unthinkably, it still exists today as a ghostly imprint in the landscape.

As an architecture student, this image haunts me because the size and scale of Auschwitz resemble that of a small town. It reveals the reality that people—families, friends, and neighbours—inhabited it. The size was necessary to amass and kill the number of innocents who died here, and helps us understand that designing such a plan was a determined undertaking. This was the last place for more than a million people before their deaths and the most horrifying home for those who survived—including my relatives.

I am the granddaughter of Polish and Russian immigrants who fled their homes; several of my distant relatives are survivors of Auschwitz. Looking at this aerial plan is looking at a part of my family's roots— we know little of their lives before the death camp. This place changed the entire course of their existence and is the closest I can come to understanding where they came from. My relatives always hid the tattooed numbers on their arms and remained painfully silent. There were no words to describe this place, what they saw, and what life was like here. We often forget that people not only died here, but they had to live here too.

My hope is that *The Evidence Room* will leave visitors awestruck and without words so that they too will understand how real, yet unimaginable, this place was, even to those who lived in it.

Preparing the moulds of drawings, photos, and letters to be cast, I've somehow both been tracing the footsteps of the people who originally created the documents and, at the same time, atoning and repenting for the wrongs that were committed. With each bit of plaster that I scrape out of a mould, and with each letter that I wash free of soot, I become intimate with the act of drawing and writing these documents. I move between wondering about the people who created documents to enable mass killing and feeling deeply saddened by the drawings created by the survivors. I sometimes spend hours poring over an image—of a woman leading a child into a gas chamber, of another being dragged out of the chamber by the neck. As I sit and patiently scrub clean a wooden mould for a letter—mirrored so that the cast comes out the right way—I think there's a certain irony. The very act of preparing the mould is the mirror image of the original. What the author wrote in ink, I scrub free of dark soot. The very thing they created for death is recreated for remembering life. What was done either without conscience or with a suppressed conscience is now worked on consciously for hours. The cast is always a reflection of the mould, and the mould is a reflection of the original. In this process of mould-making and casting, much more has been reflected and reflected on than just the image of an original.

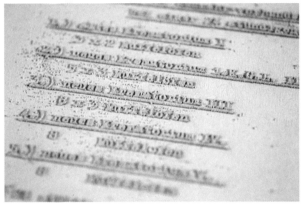

figs. 82–83

fig. 84

For four months, I worked methodically on the production of evidence casts. Repetition was key—the moulds and images changed with each cast, but the methods and procedures remained consistent to create and refine the sixty final panels. The process quickly became a fluid motion.

In our daily routines, we often slip into muscle memory where actions are no longer deliberate, settling into a comfortable rhythm that doesn't demand engagement in the moment. Within my daily casting routine, the meaning of the imagery being produced was often lost in this motion. Only when the routine was broken, in moments of interruption, challenge, or failure did the reality of the imagery push beyond the plaster. I was easily caught up in deliberations over techniques and legibility, but when I allowed myself to study the evidence being portrayed instead of the material output, I struggled to complete the task at hand.

With no evident connection to the Holocaust or Auschwitz, I found myself questioning the legitimacy of my role in *The Evidence Room*. But I realized that the Holocaust was not only a Nazi crime or a Jewish tragedy, but a human crime and a human tragedy. Day after day, my peers and I were confronted with unquestionable proof of the systematic mass murder of millions. However, it remained necessary that we continued to work effectively so that the evidence could be presented in Venice. The significance of my role was in this fluid motion—the refinement of my skills, to temporarily numb myself to the images, to produce so the world could see the human atrocities of our past.

During my second day of work on *The Evidence Room*, I was asked to revise a set of drawings. It was an ordinary task, something I had performed daily during previous internships. Without hesitation, I sat down and began. It was a few minutes before I realized exactly what I was drawing. While dimensioning the elevation, I began to understand. My cursor traced a long curved object on the front of a door and a thirty-five-centimetre tag appeared, indicating its length. I paused. I was dimensioning a latch on the door designed to seal people inside the gas chambers at Auschwitz.

The tactility of the handle jerked my emotions. An image of a prisoner's thin hand on the handle appeared, tasked with the terrible job of locking the door. The clang of steel hitting steel rang, the steel latch finding the steel catch on the doorframe as it was thrown down. A fatal clang. I imagined a mother with her two kids inside the gas chamber. I imagined what that clang meant to her and to the more than a million other humans who heard it. The panic that must have risen from their innards when they realized they were locked inside.

It was sobering to understand that my work on *The Evidence Room* would be different from any previous experience. The exhibition would reveal the design of objects that were the detailed parts of a systematic killing machine. It would illustrate the power of design and the ethical responsibility a designer must carry.

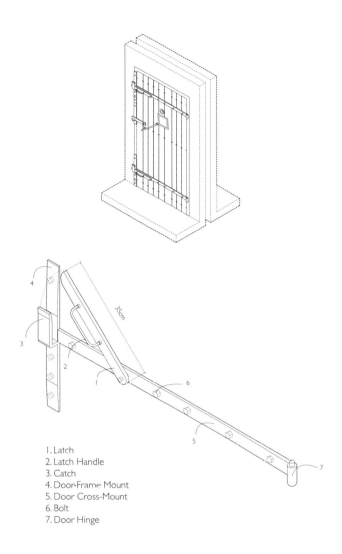

1. Latch
2. Latch Handle
3. Catch
4. Door-Frame Mount
5. Door Cross-Mount
6. Bolt
7. Door Hinge

fig. 85

The third finger of my right hand gently depresses the safety switch as my thumb cycles the operation control forward to the choke position. I prime the fuel bulb twice to ensure an ignitable mix in the carburetor. I reflect on the fact that I am using a German-manufactured chainsaw to retrieve historic timber from the bank barn of the Lapsley farm, Lot 21 on the north side of the 8th Concession in the former Beverly Township for the construction of a gastight door, a hatch, and a ladder to be displayed in Venice. The Stihl MS 250 starts on the first pull. The surgical excision of the wall studs between the upper girt and the sill beam involves a single horizontal cut to the shoulder of the timber. As the carbide-tipped chain glides through the eastern white pine intermediates, paired hand-cut mortises in the frame are exposed for the first time in 177 years.

The destruction of a method of joinery that was characteristic of an agrarian vernacular typology saddens me. Although this long-abandoned barn faces eventual demolition, it was meticulously constructed to support an ambitious Ontario farming family that relied on it to house both livestock and the toils of harvest.

The architecture of Auschwitz resonates in my mind as I load the truck with the recovered materials. The barracks and the gas chambers share a similar approach to craft with the barn—a simple method of construction built with robust local materials by a highly skilled labour force—with the distinction that the workers in Auschwitz were slave labourers. As both a carpenter and architecture student, I will repurpose the granary boards and dimensional timber into replicas of key pieces of evidence from the Irving trial for *The Evidence Room*— their original form forever lost as they are transformed from their revered place within a machine for living on the Ontario landscape into a machine for death.

fig. 86

The original drawing set for Crematorium 4 is an attentively drafted document. The lines, so clear and purposeful, make the omnipresent markings seem mechanical, cold, and heartless. It was my job to retrace this pristine depiction of Crematorium 4 for our casts.

Translating ink into black pixels, I ran my stylus across a digital tablet; I repeatedly traced doors annotated by "90/205," indicating openings 90 centimetres in width and 205 centimetres in height. Every line, hatch, and note slowly crystallized into a psychological tectonic construct of Crematorium 4 until I reached an annotation that, unexpectedly and incorrectly, read "9/205."

What happened to the "0" after the "9"? Why did the precise copy that I was tracing not register it? Was it lost behind eraser markings? Was it smudged into previous iterations of the wall hosting it?

This inaccuracy shattered the walls, buckled the columns, and distorted the lines that represented the making of Crematorium 4 inside my head. This miniscule fault revealed the grand truth—this mistake was human and the flesh of the hand that authored this murdering machine was imprinted on the vellum. Anger and disbelief followed—anger with the architect behind the markings that made up this cruel construction and disbelief because this architect shared the same human traits as all of us—forgetfulness and error.

As I worked on this project, which presents architecture as evidence of the Holocaust, I realized just how fragile and precious details are. The absence of the "0" after the "9" is what *The Evidence Room* attempts to prevent. The presence of the "0" after the "9" is what *The Evidence Room* stands for. It is important for humanity to trace an unequivocal picture of its past to remember, as humans, that we are capable of anything.

fig. 87 →

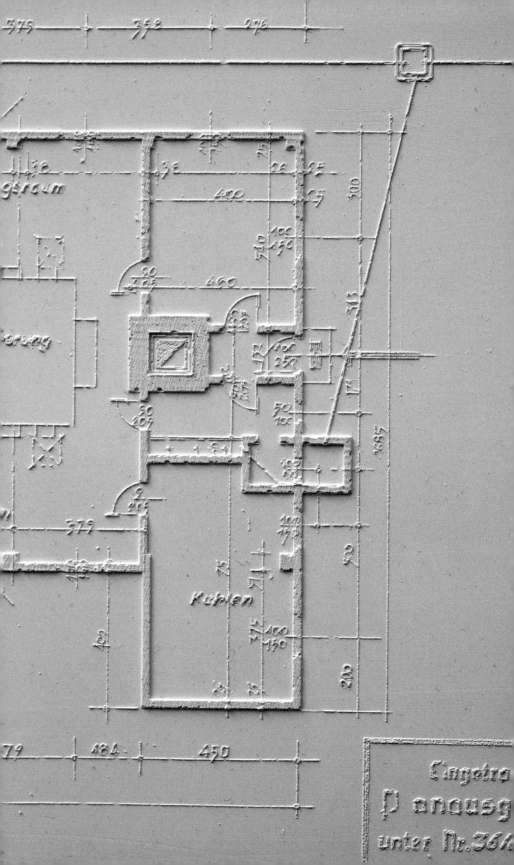

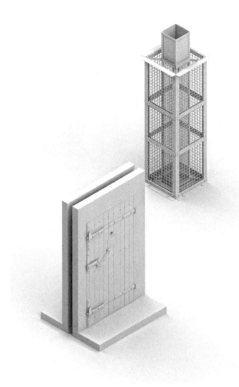

fig. 88

fig. 89

fig. 90

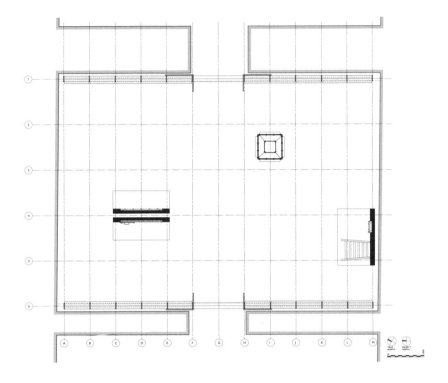

fig. 91

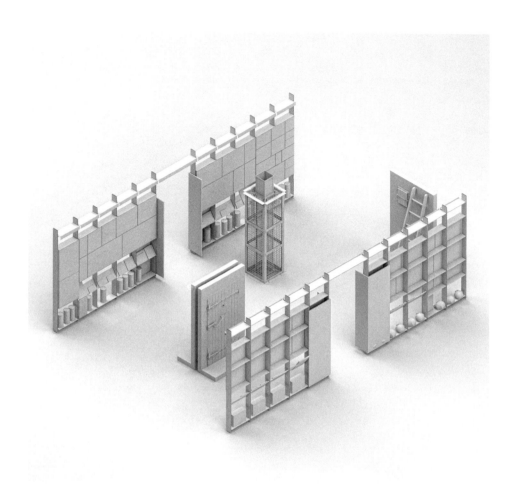

fig. 92

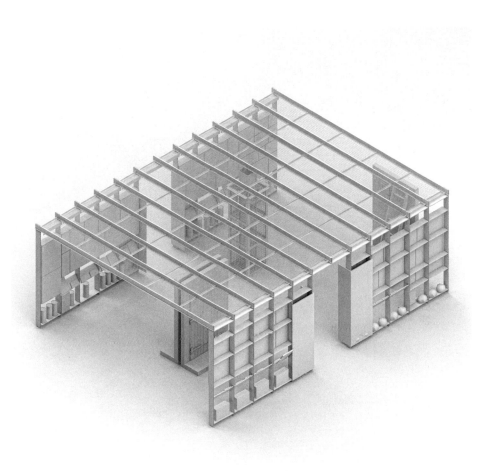

fig. 93

fig. 94

# List of figures

1. The architects, draftsmen, and construction managers of the Auschwitz Central Construction Management gathered on the porch of their office, 1943. These men deliberately designed the Auschwitz gas chambers and crematoria as factories of death. COURTESY ARCHIVE AUSCHWITZ-BIRKENAU MEMORIAL AND MUSEUM, OŚWIĘCIM.

2. Crematorium 4 shortly after completion, Spring 1943. The three gas chambers were located in the lower part, farthest from the incineration room. This building had an official cremation capacity of 768 corpses per day. COURTESY ARCHIVE AUSCHWITZ-BIRKENAU MEMORIAL AND MUSEUM, OŚWIĘCIM.

3. A gastight door with a peephole found by Russian troops in the building materials stockyard of the camp in 1945. This side of the door was the one facing the victims and hence did not show the two latches. The peephole was protected on the victim side by a hemispherical metal grid. PHOTO: UNKNOWN RUSSIAN PHOTOGRAPHER. COURTESY ARCHIVE AUSCHWITZ-BIRKENAU MEMORIAL AND MUSEUM, OŚWIĘCIM.

4. Two gas shutters measuring 30 cm by 40 cm found in 1945 at Crematorium 5 and stored, when this photo was taken in 1999, in the coke room of Crematorium 1. PHOTO: OMER ARBEL.

5. Tins of Zyklon-B discovered in the Majdanek concentration camp. MAIN COMMISSION FOR THE PROSECUTION OF THE CRIMES AGAINST THE POLISH NATION, COURTESY PHOTO ARCHIVES UNITED STATES HOLOCAUST MEMORIAL MUSEUM, WASHINGTON D.C.

6. Plan of Auschwitz-Birkenau drawn in February 1943. This plan is the first that shows the final locations of Crematoria 2, 3, 4, and 5. Certain main buildings, like the large guardhouse shielding Crematoria 4 and 5 from view from the major east-west camp road, were never constructed. This plan, the original of which is in the archive of the Auschwitz-Birkenau Memorial and Museum, Oświęcim, was redrawn in the early 1990s for publication by Mikolaj Kadlubowski. COURTESY ROBERT JAN VAN PELT.

7. Plan and elevation of Crematorium 4, January 1943. In the plan, drawn by SS architect Walter Dejaco, the three gas chambers are depicted on the left, while in the elevation, they can be seen on the right. The three small windows in the low wing containing the gas chambers are the apertures through which the Zyklon-B was inserted into the gas chambers. These apertures measured 34 cm by 40 cm. This plan, the original of which is in the archive of the Auschwitz-Birkenau Memorial and Museum, Oświęcim, was redrawn in the early 1990s for publication by Mikolaj Kadlubowski. COURTESY ROBERT JAN VAN PELT.

8. The hemispherical grid protecting the peephole on the inside of a gastight door found by soldiers of the Red Army in 1945. COURTESY ARCHIVE AUSCHWITZ-BIRKENAU MEMORIAL AND MUSEUM, OŚWIĘCIM.

9. Detail of the plan of Crematorium 4 showing parts of two of the three gas chambers. Visible are the gastight doors that open outward and the 30-by-40 cm apertures through which the Zyklon-B was inserted into the gas chambers. COURTESY ARCHIVE AUSCHWITZ-BIRKENAU MEMORIAL AND MUSEUM, OŚWIĘCIM.

10. Interior of the office of the Auschwitz Central Construction Management, 1943. COURTESY ARCHIVE AUSCHWITZ-BIRKENAU MEMORIAL AND MUSEUM, OŚWIĘCIM.

11. Memorandum of a meeting held in the Auschwitz Central Construction Management, August 19, 1942. This document discusses the construction of two crematoria (later to be numbered 4 and 5) near "bathhouses for special actions." These so-called "bathhouses," known as Bunkers 1 and 2, were peasant cottages that had been modified into gas chambers.

Courtesy Archive Auschwitz-Birkenau
Memorial and Museum, Oświęcim.

12. Letter from Karl Bischoff to the German
Armament Works, March 31, 1943. This letter
mentions that three gastight doors should
be made following the design of such doors
already delivered for Crematoria 4 and 5. In
addition it reminds the addressee of an order
for a gastight door measuring 100 cm wide
and 192 cm high, "to be made with a spyhole
of double 8 mm glass with a rubber seal and a
metal fitting. This order must be considered as
very urgent." Courtesy Archive Auschwitz-
Birkenau Memorial and Museum, Oświęcim.

13. Order of February 13, 1942, for Crematoria 4
and 5 issued by the Auschwitz Central
Construction Office to the German Armament
Works. The order is for the "production of
12 gastight doors approximately 30/40 cm
exactly as those already made in the inmates'
woodworking shop, with bolt and catch."
Courtesy Archive Auschwitz-Birkenau
Memorial and Museum, Oświęcim.

14. Detail of the section of the gas chamber
of Crematorium 4, showing the gas hatch.
Courtesy Archive Auschwitz-Birkenau
Memorial and Museum, Oświęcim.

15. Detail of the plan of Crematorium 4, show-
ing the gastight door. Courtesy Archive
Auschwitz-Birkenau Memorial and
Museum, Oświęcim.

16. Detail of one of the three gas chambers of
Crematorium 4 showing one of the 30-by-
40 cm apertures through which the Zyklon-B
was inserted into the gas chambers. Courtesy
Archive Auschwitz-Birkenau Memorial
and Museum, Oświęcim.

17. Inspection by members of the Polish forensic
commission of the entrance to the ruined
undressing room of Crematorium 2. Courtesy

Archive Auschwitz-Birkenau Memorial
and Museum, Oświęcim.

18. Reconstruction of the killing installation of
Crematorium 2 made in 1945. To the left are
the stairs leading to the entrance (wchod) of the
underground undressing room (rozbieralnia),
which connects to the gas chamber (komora
gazowa). The Zyklon-B was introduced through
four poison-introduction devices (wsyp trucizny).
Courtesy Archive Auschwitz-Birkenau
Memorial and Museum, Oświęcim.

19. The ovens of Crematorium 2, shortly before
their completion, January 1943. Courtesy
Archive Auschwitz-Birkenau Memorial
and Museum, Oświęcim.

20. Tins of Zyklon-B discovered in the Majdanek
concentration camp. Main Commission for
the Prosecution of the Crimes against the
Polish Nation, courtesy Photo Archives
United States Holocaust Memorial
Museum, Washington D.C.

21. Remains of a ventilation duct in the east wall
of the gas chamber of Crematorium 3, 1999.
Photo: Omer Arbel.

22. Ground floor of Crematorium 2, January 1942.
The five triple-muffle ovens, with an official cremation capacity of 1,440 corpses per day, can be
seen in the large central room. Three forced-draft
ventilators can be seen adjacent to the chimney.
This plan, the original of which is in the archive
of the Auschwitz-Birkenau Memorial and
Museum, Oświęcim, was redrawn in the early
1990s for publication by Mikolaj Kadlubowski.
Courtesy Robert Jan van Pelt.

23. Section of Crematorium 2, January 1942.
The triple-muffle incinerator (left) and the
trash incinerator (right) are connected to the
chimney by underground flues. Adjacent to
the chimney is one of the three forced-draft
ventilators (each ventilator is connected to two

flues). Each of these ventilators was placed in a small room that became very hot when the crematorium was in operation. In a letter of March 6, 1943, Auschwitz chief architect Karl Bischoff proposed to recycle the heat of these rooms into "morgue 1"—clearly to facilitate the evaporation of the hydrogen cyanide from the Zyklon-B pellets. The drawing also shows sections of both morgue 1, which became a gas chamber, and morgue 2, which became an undressing room. The section of the former shows ventilation systems built into the walls. COURTESY ARCHIVE AUSCHWITZ-BIRKENAU MEMORIAL AND MUSEUM, OŚWIĘCIM.

24. Fragment of elevation of Crematorium 2, January 1942. This drawing provides a section view through morgue 1 at the point where the ventilation shafts in the walls are connected by ducts that transverse above and below the chamber. COURTESY ARCHIVE AUSCHWITZ-BIRKENAU MEMORIAL AND MUSEUM, OŚWIĘCIM.

25. View of Crematorium 3, drawn by Auschwitz survivor Yehuda Bacon, 1945. The drawing shows the outside staircase to the basement constructed during the completion of the building to facilitate access to the gas chamber. The drawing also shows the roof of the gas chamber (top left), with the four covers of the gas columns. COURTESY YAD VASHEM AND YEHUDA BACON, JERUSALEM.

26. View of the gas chamber of Crematorium 3, drawn by Auschwitz survivor Yehuda Bacon, 1945. Bacon's attempt to draw an axonometric representation of the gas chamber shows the hollow gas column in the centre with its wooden cover. He made a second drawing of the plan of the wooden cover in the top left corner of the drawing. Bacon also showed the fake shower heads and the lights with their wire-mesh protective covers. A keen observer, he correctly remembered the almost barrel--vault appearance of the ceiling of the gas chamber caused by the ventilation ducts located

against the ceiling. COURTESY YAD VASHEM AND YEHUDA BACON, JERUSALEM.

27. Letter from Karl Bischoff to Hans Kammler, June 29, 1943. In this letter the chief architect of the Auschwitz Central Construction Management reports to his boss in Berlin that, with the completion of Crematorium 3, Auschwitz is equipped with crematoria that have a total daily incineration capacity of 4,756 corpses. COURTESY RUSSIAN STATE MILITARY ARCHIVE, MOSCOW.

28. Letter from Karl Bischoff to Topf and Sons, February 11, 1943. This letter berates Topf for the delay in the delivery of a "No. 450 blower with a 3.5 horsepower motor, and it is precisely this blower destined for morgue 1 which we need most urgently." The blower was to allow the room to be ventilated after the gassing. COURTESY ARCHIVE AUSCHWITZ-BIRKENAU MEMORIAL AND MUSEUM, OŚWIĘCIM.

29. Letter from Karl Bischoff to Topf and Sons, March 6, 1943. In this letter, the chief architect of the Auschwitz Central Construction Management informs Topf and Sons that "In accordance with your proposal, the department agrees that morgue 1 will be preheated with the air coming from the rooms with the three installations that generate the forced draught." Preheating makes no sense in the context of a morgue, but was essential for a Zyklon-B gas chamber. COURTESY ARCHIVE AUSCHWITZ-BIRKENAU MEMORIAL AND MUSEUM, OŚWIĘCIM.

30. Memorandum of a meeting held at the Auschwitz Central Construction Management, January 29, 1943. This document covers the problems generated by the inability of the contractors to obtain heavy-duty circuit breakers for Crematorium 2. The electrical engineer suggests that, until such breakers are obtained, one can only consider "a limited use of the available machines (allowing for simultaneous burning and Special Treatment) because the main electricity supply is not able to carry its power

consumption." Under the Nazi regime, "Special Treatment" was code for murder. COURTESY RUSSIAN STATE MILITARY ARCHIVE, MOSCOW.

31. The memoirs of Rudolf Höss, 1946. In his memoirs, written in a Polish jail, former Auschwitz Commandant Rudolf Höss discussed the genocidal intention and operation of the Auschwitz crematoria in detail. COURTESY ARCHIVE AUSCHWITZ-BIRKENAU MEMORIAL AND MUSEUM, OŚWIĘCIM.

32. Rudolf Höss in Polish captivity, 1946. COURTESY ARCHIVE AUSCHWITZ-BIRKENAU MEMORIAL AND MUSEUM, OŚWIĘCIM.

33. Aerial photograph of the south and central part of Auschwitz-Birkenau, taken on August 25, 1944. The photograph shows Crematoria 2, 3, 4, and 5. COURTESY NATIONAL ARCHIVES, WASHINGTON D.C.

34. Detail of aerial photograph of Auschwitz-Birkenau, taken on August 25, 1944, showing Crematoria 2 and 3. COURTESY NATIONAL ARCHIVES, WASHINGTON D.C.

35. Detail of aerial photograph of Auschwitz-Birkenau, taken on August 25, 1944, showing Crematorium 3. The zigzag formation of the four dots on the roof of the gas chamber matches eyewitness descriptions of the location of the four gas columns. COURTESY NATIONAL ARCHIVES, WASHINGTON D.C.

36. Photograph of Crematorium 2, taken from the south, December 1942. COURTESY ARCHIVE AUSCHWITZ-BIRKENAU MEMORIAL AND MUSEUM, OŚWIĘCIM.

37. Detail photograph of Crematorium 2, taken from the south, December 1942. The top of the gas chamber can be seen just to the right of the locomotive's chimney. The concrete roof is not yet covered with dirt and therefore the tops of the four gas columns can be seen. COURTESY

ARCHIVE AUSCHWITZ-BIRKENAU MEMORIAL AND MUSEUM, OŚWIĘCIM.

38. Aerial photograph of the Auschwitz area, taken on June 26, 1944. The photograph shows, from top to bottom, Auschwitz-Birkenau, the railway corridor with the Auschwitz station, the Auschwitz *Stammlager* (main camp), the Sola river as it flows into the Vistula river (right), the town of Auschwitz, and the large IG Farben plant. COURTESY NATIONAL ARCHIVES, WASHINGTON D.C.

39. Back elevation and basement of a new crematorium to be built in Auschwitz, fall 1941. Architect Georg Werkmann. A modified version of this design was ultimately constructed in Auschwitz-Birkenau as Crematorium 2 and a mirror version of it as Crematorium 3. The basement shows the original arrangement of two morgues. One was to become an undressing room and one a gas chamber. COURTESY RUSSIAN STATE MILITARY ARCHIVE, MOSCOW.

40. Front elevation and main floor of a new crematorium to be built in Auschwitz, fall 1941. Architect Georg Werkmann. COURTESY RUSSIAN STATE MILITARY ARCHIVE, MOSCOW.

41. Situation sketch of the location of the *Stammlager* and railway corridor, Auschwitz-Birkenau, and the birch forest west of Auschwitz-Birkenau. This drawing was made by Auschwitz escapees Rudolf Vrba and Alfred Wetzler in April 1944. It was published six month later in the first full report on the Auschwitz factory of death. WAR REFUGEE BOARD, *THE EXTERMINATION CAMPS OF AUSCHWITZ (OSWIECIM) AND BIRKENAU IN UPPER SILESIA* (1944).

42. Vrba and Wetzler's plan of Auschwitz-Birkenau, showing the location of the four crematoria. All the crematoria are, erroneously, depicted as identical structures. WAR REFUGEE BOARD, *THE EXTERMINATION CAMPS OF AUSCHWITZ (OSWIECIM) AND BIRKENAU IN UPPER SILESIA* (1944).

main floor, with exception of the autopsy rooms located above the two vestibules in the basement (no. 2 and the unnumbered space adjacent to the SS entrance to the basement). COURTESY BET LOHAMEI HAGETAOT MUSEUM, KIBBUTZ LOHAMEI HAGETAOT.

57. Incineration room of Crematorium 3, drawn by David Olère, 1945. COURTESY BET LOHAMEI HAGETAOT MUSEUM, KIBBUTZ LOHAMEI HAGETAOT.

58. Basement plan of Crematorium 2, January 1942. At this time, the two large basement rooms were still intended as morgues. The main access to the basement was by means of a corpse slide. COURTESY ARCHIVE AUSCHWITZ-BIRKENAU MEMORIAL AND MUSEUM, OŚWIĘCIM.

59. Modification of the basement of Crematorium 2, Fall 1942. This plan shows the removal of the corpse slide, the construction of a new staircase connecting the outside to the basement, and doors to one of the two morgues that now open outward. COURTESY ARCHIVE AUSCHWITZ-BIRKENAU MEMORIAL AND MUSEUM, OŚWIĘCIM.

60. Detail of the basement of the original plan of the large crematorium designed for Auschwitz, October 1941. The door to morgue 1 opens inward. Also clearly visible are the slide and the adjacent stairways. COURTESY RUSSIAN STATE MILITARY ARCHIVE, MOSCOW.

61. Detail of the basement of the second plan of this crematorium, which will be built as Crematorium 2 in Auschwitz-Birkenau, January 1942. While it is difficult to see, as the architect rubbed out the lines showing the door panels, it is still possible to determine that in this plan the doors to morgue 1 open inward. Also clearly visible are the slide and the adjacent stairways. COURTESY ARCHIVE AUSCHWITZ-BIRKENAU MEMORIAL AND MUSEUM, OŚWIĘCIM.

62. Detail of the basement of the final modification of Crematorium 2, Fall 1942. The doors to morgue 1 now open outward. COURTESY ARCHIVE AUSCHWITZ-BIRKENAU MEMORIAL AND MUSEUM, OŚWIĘCIM.

63. Section of Crematorium 3, drawn by David Olère, 1946. Olère provided the drawing with a numbered key to identify the parts, and a legend. For the sake of making comparison easier, I have also included, where relevant, the number that Olère used to indicate that same building part in the plan reproduced above. NB: Olère represented the gas chamber (D/3), which projected outward to the north of the building at the back and would have been hidden by the vestibule, under the incineration room (which had no basement). (A/1) undressing room; (B) cell; (C/4) corpse elevator; (D/3) gas chamber; (E/10) [metal] grate [columns] for gas bombs; (F) SS: lethal experiments and dissection; (G) entry for SS; (H/0) incinerator; (I/12) coal truck; (J/9) SS guards; (K/7) chimney; (L) quarters of the crematorium slaves; (M) those who disentangle hair; (N) casters, jewels, teeth, gold; (O) forced air ventilator; (P) smoke extractor; (Q) outside view. COURTESY BET LOHAMEI HAGETAOT MUSEUM, KIBBUTZ LOHAMEI HAGETAOT.

64. Gas column, Version 4, which—in terms of materials, dimensions, profiles—was the originally proposed column construction, developed after considering any earlier interpretations, the original, thin graphic evidence from surviving documents and reports, and drawings from survivors. DRAWING: DONALD MCKAY.

65. Gas column, Version 6, close to the final column built for *The Evidence Room*. Version 6 incorporates construction details based on the steelworkers' research into "good practice" circa 1940. DRAWING: DONALD MCKAY AND MICHAEL NUGENT.

66. Making the wire mesh panels for the outer cage of the gas. The metal twisted and warped from the heat of welding so it needed to be held in place by a heavy jig. PHOTO: MICHAEL NUGENT.

# List of figures (continued)

81. Aerial photograph of Auschwitz-Birkenau taken in August 1944. The grounds of the camp cover nearly four square kilometres. Crematoria 2, 3, 4, and 5 are located on the eastern edge of the site and the central grid plan of the grounds shows the barracks where men, women, and (very occasionally) children lived before their deaths. COURTESY NATIONAL ARCHIVES, WASHINGTON D.C.

82. Anna Beznogova cleaning soot from a basswood mould of a letter. PHOTO: ANNA BEZNOGOVA.

83. Close-up photograph showing a cast of the letter from Karl Bischoff to Hans Kammler of June 29, 1943, which lists the official incineration capacity of the Auschwitz crematoria (see fig. 27). PHOTO: ANNA BEZNOGOVA.

84. Anna Beznogova and Anna Longrigg preparing a mould made from a laser-cut acrylic panel that will be filled with Hydrocal drywall cement, prepared with water at specific volumes to produce a rigid, embossed cast. This image captures an early moment of discovery that established the best practice used to produce the casts sent to Venice. PHOTO: PIPER BERNBAUM.

85. Axonometric drawing of the gastight door monument and detail showing the gastight door latch. DRAWING: SIOBHAN ALLMAN.

86. Bradley Paddock removing pine studs that will be used to make the gastight door and the gas hatch. PHOTO: CARRIE PADDOCK.

87. Detail of an early trial cast of the plan of Crematorium 4 showing a missing "0" in the door annotation (see fig. 7). CAST: SIOBHAN ALLMAN, ANNA BEZNOGOVA, ANNE BORDELEAU, ANNA LONGRIGG, ALEXANDRU VILCU. PHOTO: FRED HUNSBERGER.

88. The three monuments: the gastight door (front and back), the gas hatch (front), and the gas column, as they are arranged in *The Evidence Room*. DRAWING: SIOBHAN ALLMAN, ANNA LONGRIGG, DONALD MCKAY, MICHAEL NUGENT, NICOLE RATAJCZAK, ALEXANDRU VILCU.

89. View of *The Evidence Room* looking west, showing the gas column and the west wall exhibits. DRAWING: SIOBHAN ALLMAN, ANNA LONGRIGG, DONALD MCKAY, MICHAEL NUGENT, NICOLE RATAJCZAK, ALEXANDRU VILCU.

90. View of *The Evidence Room* looking west, showing the back of the gastight door and the west wall exhibits. DRAWING: SIOBHAN ALLMAN, ANNA LONGRIGG, DONALD MCKAY, MICHAEL NUGENT, NICOLE RATAJCZAK, ALEXANDRU VILCU.

91. Plan of *The Evidence Room* showing the three monuments and the matrix of shelves on the east and west walls that support the plaster exhibits. DRAWING: DONALD MCKAY.

92. The three monuments and the east and west walls of shelves as they are arranged in *The Evidence Room*. DRAWING: SIOBHAN ALLMAN, ANNA LONGRIGG, DONALD MCKAY, MICHAEL NUGENT, NICOLE RATAJCZAK, ALEXANDRU VILCU.

93. The three monuments, the east and west walls of shelves, and the ceiling of the room as they are arranged in *The Evidence Room*. DRAWING: SIOBHAN ALLMAN, ANNA LONGRIGG, DONALD MCKAY, MICHAEL NUGENT, NICOLE RATAJCZAK, ALEXANDRU VILCU.

94. View of *The Evidence Room* looking east, showing the front face of the gastight door, the gas column, the gastight hatch and ladder, and the east wall exhibits. DRAWING: SIOBHAN ALLMAN, ANNA LONGRIGG, DONALD MCKAY, MICHAEL NUGENT, NICOLE RATAJCZAK, ALEXANDRU VILCU.

*Hineni*: An Essay in Acknowledgment
– Robert Jan van Pelt

הנני or *hineni*, in English "Here I am," is one of the key words in
the Hebrew Bible. When God called Abraham, he responded with
"hineni," laying himself open to the no-matter-what-might-come.
"Here I am," and not a mere "I'm here." When God called Moses, he
also responded with "hineni." With that word, Abraham and Moses
put themselves unconditionally under obligation.

Writing in the wake of the Holocaust, when so many turned away
while their Jewish neighbours—"the other"—were loaded into depor-
tation trains, French philosopher Emmanuel Levinas articulated an
understanding of human existence based on the recognition that none
of us is alone, that each of us becomes only fully human—a *Mensch*—
through the encounter with another person, someone who is, in the
first instance, always a stranger. In this meeting, we respond to the
stranger's call with a "hineni," bearing witness to the other.

In the past six months the word *hineni* often crossed my mind.
It did so first on July 28, 2015, when I received an email from
Alejandro Aravena, inviting me to join him in the 15th Venice
Architecture Biennale by contributing an exhibition on my forensic
work on the architecture of Auschwitz. The *hineni* did not so much
apply to my own enthusiastic acceptance of his invitation—after
all, a refusal was unthinkable—but to his response to a book I
had written as an expert witness on the design, construction, and
operation of the Auschwitz extermination camp in a notorious libel
trial. In 2007, I shared dinner with Alejandro after a lecture he gave
at the University of Waterloo School of Architecture in Cambridge,
Ontario. Impressed with the ethical and imaginative dimension
of his architectural practice, I offered him a copy of *The Case for
Auschwitz: Evidence from the Irving Trial* (2002). In an email, he
thanked me for having testified and for having written it, noting,
"Now I feel some depth in the way we should behave as human
beings." I recognized in this first email a *hineni* to the terrible history
I had written, which described the greatest ethical fall in the history
of the architectural profession. And I recognized a same *hineni* in the
second email I received from him, seven years later. With the once-
in-a-lifetime opportunity of curating a Venice Architecture Biennale,
Alejandro did not shy away from placing the black hole that is
Auschwitz at the core of his exhibition.

Having accepted Alejandro's invitation—which came with the
stipulation of secrecy until late February 2016—I discretely sought
help, knowing well that I needed much of it: after all, I could not
simply paste the pages of *The Case for Auschwitz* on the walls of

Room Q in the Central Pavilion. My wife, Miriam, accepted the inconvenient intrusion of the Biennale into our already fully filled life and her critical acumen, wise counsel, and faith in the enterprise meant, on more than one occasion, the difference between giving up and continuing. My colleague and friend Donald McKay immediately and unreservedly responded to my call for help. During lunch on August 7, Donald, Miriam, and I imagined what became *The Evidence Room.* The exhibition in Venice would include a replica of a Zyklon-B gas column, a gastight door with a peephole, and other replicas of evidence of the genocidal purpose of the Auschwitz gas chambers and ovens. During that meeting Donald offered to sacrifice a sabbatical, meant to support his own creative work, and accepted responsibility for the design and production of the exhibition.

It was a given for us that this project ought to emerge from Waterloo Architecture, where Donald had taught for almost forty years and I for twenty-eight. Personally, it meant an opportunity to express my gratitude for the fact that when, in the mid-1980s, I began my work on the architectural history of the German extermination camps, only Waterloo Architecture recognized its relevance. Through its Cultural History curriculum, created, maintained, and expanded by Larry Cummings, Robert Wiljer, and Rick Haldenby, students confronted the architects' role in the Holocaust long before I showed up for my job interview.

At the end of August, Donald and I invited our colleague Anne Bordeleau to join the project. By that time it had become clear that the exhibition involved plaster casts and Anne had both researched casting as a theoretical issue and engaged it in workshops as an artistic practice. She wholeheartedly accepted responsibility for designing and producing the plaster exhibits. By the time we established our troika, I had already talked to Sascha Hastings, who had helped mount three Biennale exhibitions in the Canada Pavilion in Venice. Sascha knew what we could expect in Venice and immediately put her experience at our disposal, accepting increased responsibility as time progressed, challenges mounted, and it became apparent that we needed an editor for this book. In November she officially joined the enterprise, turning the troika into a four-in-hand.

If Miriam and the core team provided the driving force, many friends, colleagues, acquaintances, and even strangers helped us realize *The Evidence Room.* Early on, Dachau survivor Elly Gotz—who, as a seventeen-year-old slave labourer involved in the construction of a giant, underground bomb-proof aircraft factory, and later as a pro-fessional engineer, has a good sense of what should and should not be made—gave his approval to the project. He also generously wrote the preface to this book.

At the University of Waterloo, many provided help—practical, moral, and spiritual. Interim Associate Vice President, International, Jean-Jacques van Vlasselaer became a tireless advocate for the project inside and outside the university, and Dean Pearl Sullivan and Vice President George Dixon underwrote, with matching funds, a projected grant from the Social Sciences and Humanities Research Council (SSHRC). Tom Barber helped us shape the application. Realizing the very short timeframe available, Interim Vice President, Advancement, Erin Sargeant Greenwood and Mike den Haan assigned the project priority status in the Office of Advancement. Bonnie Fay Oberle energetically and faithfully managed the file, while Nenone Donaldson took care of any Venice business within the Faculty of Engineering. At Waterloo Architecture, Lola Sheppard, Rick Haldenby, Lorenzo Pignatti, Sarah Nichols, Mona Skuterud, Fred Hunsberger, Matt Oliver, Heinz Kohler, and Dan Jessel made themselves available to help us overcome the problems we faced on the ground.

Close coordination with Alejandro's office in Santiago, Chile, and with the Biennale office in Venice, was vital to the success of *The Evidence Room*. Agustina Labarca in Santiago, and Marina Bertaggia, Joern Brandmeyer, Gerardo Cejas, Sandra Durand de la Penne, Manuela Lucà-Dazio, Sandra Montagner, and Luigi Ricciari in Venice provided us with feedback whenever asked and helped us negotiate our unprecedented problem—mounting an exhibition almost 7,000 kilometres away in a matter of months.

Early on, Mirko Zardini of the Canadian Centre for Architecture in Montreal offered to host a smaller, parallel exhibition on the forensic interpretation of the Auschwitz gas chambers and crematoria. We were glad for this opportunity to mount our work in one of the most distinguished architectural museums in the world, and look forward to our collaboration with him and his colleagues Giovanna Borasi, Delphine Lesage, and Sébastien Larivière.

In the fledgling months of the project, Miriam and I, Miriam's aunt Bernadette Rosenstadt, our colleague Elizabeth English, and my friend and neighbour Stephen Otto primed the fundraising pump, allowing us to commission a survey of Room Q and produce fundraising brochures. Initially, these seemed to have little effect; many promising avenues of funding turned out to be dead-ends. By mid-November 2015, it appeared that the project would collapse. At that time, Waterloo Architecture student Michael Nugent, his father, Tom Nugent, and Tom's friend Bob Intini volunteered to construct two copies of the key monument, the steel Zyklon-B gas column—one for Venice and one for the Montreal exhibition. We accepted their offer in a meeting at Bob's plant in Hamilton. This proved to be the green light for Venice.

In early December, University of Waterloo Professor Emeritus Paul

Socken and Bruce Kuwabara—founding partner of KPMB Architects and one of Canada's leading architects—embraced the project. Paul was committed to Jewish Studies and Bruce, whose parents and their entire families on both sides were interned with 22,000 other Canadians of Japanese descent during World War II in a Canadian internment camp, immediately understood that *The Evidence Room* was vitally important. In a remarkable coincidence, Paul presented the project to Allan Weinbaum; Bruce, on the same day, but unbeknownst to Paul, spoke with Allan's sister, Carol. The next day the Weinbaum siblings compared notes and decided to help us secure the future of the project through a gift from the Jack Weinbaum Family Foundation, established by their father, a concentration camp survivor who had immigrated to Canada.

On the third day of Hanukah—the Jewish festival that celebrates a miracle in which a small cup of oil, sufficient to light the menorah for a single day, lit the candelabra for seven more—Bruce told me that Toronto philanthropist Gerald Schwartz and his wife, Heather Reisman, through the Gerald Schwartz & Heather Reisman Foundation, had made a very substantial lead gift to the project. Suddenly, our stress acquired manageable proportions. In response to the Schwartz-Reisman gift, Acting Dean of Engineering Wayne Parker approved the funds promised by Sullivan to support student involvement in the project.

In the two months that followed, Anneke Boot and former student Ian Hill, through his firm Evans Bertrand Hill Wheeler Architecture, made contributions and Ian introduced *The Evidence Room* to the Ontario Association of Architects, which also wrote a cheque, as did the Royal Architectural Institute of Canada. Carol Weinbaum shared her own enthusiasm with her friends and so convinced Florence Minz and Marwan Osseiran to join the effort. Waterloo Architecture graduate Omer Arbel and his business partner, Randy Bishop, offered for auction one of the beautiful chandeliers that has made their firm, Bocci, a powerhouse of Canadian design world-wide. Two prominent Toronto art collectors and philanthropists joined the effort by offering major support: Sandy Simpson, under-standing the significance of the project after a meeting in Carol's home, found her way to *The Evidence Room* and David Mirvish learned about it from Bruce. Bruce's firm, KPMB Architects, also made a generous contribution and inspired by Bruce's advocacy for the project and his generosity, Jonathan and Susan Wener, and Mark and Lindy Mandelbaum joined our collective effort. Luis Ferreiro and Josean Mugica of Musealia, a Spanish company cur-rently producing a travelling exhibition on the history of Auschwitz (to open in Madrid in fall 2016), pledged a substantial cash dona-tion in exchange for the right to use, in Madrid and subsequent venues, the Zyklon-B gas column and the gastight door made for the Montreal exhibition. Finally, news arrived that the SSHRC would support our project.

And so fabrication began: we commissioned MCM in Toronto to create the steel shelving system—the so-called "matrix"—that lines the walls of Room Q, holding the plaster cast exhibits and creating the space of *The Evidence Room*. MCM's founder Gregory Rybak and his collaborators Oleg Izvekov and Robert Papka, sympathetic to the meaning of the project, gave it their all. In getting the exhibition to Venice, we received an understanding ear from Eitan Mazor and Ashton Waters at DHL Global Forwarding, which offered us generous air-freight terms at cost. Waterloo graduate Louis-Charles Lasnier took on the graphic design of this book. My literary agent, Beverley Slopen, brought us to Malcolm Lester, co-publisher of the New Jewish Press. It took one meeting between Sascha and Malcolm to suggest that this book might have a home there and, we hope, a future beyond Venice. Malcolm presented the project to his co-publisher Andrea Fochs Knight and they convinced their editorial board to sign off on the project—despite the very short timeline available to bring the book together and into the Biennale bookshop.

Like all projects, this one had to engage the triple constraint of cost, time, and quality. As we began to run out of time, with the shipping date for the exhibition coming ever closer, costs began to rise. Just when it appeared that we would run out of funds, Allan Teramura, who saw a parallel between our work and his own investigations into the camp as a tool of repression in Canada, decided to help us with a donation. At the same time, Tom and Sasha Weisz dropped by at Bob's workshop in Hamilton to see the completed gas column and they almost instantaneously decided to support the project. Finally, we discovered that a seedling, planted by Jean-Jacques early in our enterprise, had grown into a sturdy tree bearing fruit. He had told his friend Sharon Azrieli about our project and a week ago I received an email from her with a crisp message: "Whatever money is lacking you shall have." The Azrieli Foundation, which has supported both Holocaust remembrance and architectural education, was in.

From the outset we decided the project had to be the product of Waterloo Architecture. Since its founding in 1967, year after year, a new cohort of students arrives in our school, fresh-faced, eager, and innocent. The key idea of education is not only that we offer each student the necessary tools to become an architect and an educated person, but also that we prepare that student for an inheritance that is both beautiful and uplifting, as represented by Rome (where Waterloo Architecture has maintained a studio since 1979 for fourth-year students to study for a term), and terrible and terrifying, as represented by Auschwitz. In my own classes, I try to explain why they might emulate Francesco Borromini, who helped shape the face of Baroque Rome, and why they should do everything in their power not to follow the path of Walter Dejaco, who constructed the Auschwitz crematoria. And the first step toward that goal is, of course, to remember what Dejaco built and to study his work in detail.

In the past, many students did more than simply absorb the lessons offered by the crematoria. Peter Gallagher, Paul Backewich, Kate Mullin, Jed Braithwaite, and Marc Downing helped me in my attempts to reconstruct the history of Auschwitz. In the early 1990s, the late Mikolaj Kadlubowski assisted as a translator in Poland and provided at that time what turned out to be an invaluable service for *The Evidence Room* team today by faithfully tracing key architectural drawings from the Auschwitz archives.

We were extraordinarily fortunate to find students who each, in his or her own way, responded to our call. In the early phases of the project, Nicole Ratajczak produced renderings for the fundraising brochures and fourth-year students Jake Read and Fysal Amirzada travelled from Rome to Venice to survey Room Q. Later in the project, Jake helped set up the website and Carol Kaifosh, Patrick Verkley, and Quinn Greer joined the mould-making team.

At the beginning of 2016, a remarkable team of students started work in a spacious, cheerful studio room, in the workshop at Waterloo Architecture, and in the uniquely equipped private workshop of their fellow graduate student Wade Brown, generously made available to us. I supervise Piper Bernbaum's master's thesis—very impressed both by her amazing capacity to resolve the most difficult of problems and by her relentless good cheer, I knew Bernbaum should be involved. Graduate student Anna Beznogova (to be known as Anna B) had participated in one of Anne's casting workshops and the two had continued to compare notes on various techniques. We all agreed that nobody in Southwest Ontario was a better craftsman in wood than graduate student Bradley Paddock, who had also worked on one of the exhibitions in the Canada Pavilion in Venice. Piper, Anna B, and Bradley joined the team as research assistants, assuming critical roles in organizing the difficult logistics (Piper), the production of the plaster casts (Anna B), and the gastight door and gas hatch (Bradley).

Waterloo Architecture is a co-op program, meaning that undergraduate students have to complete several four-month work terms. We decided to hire four of these undergraduates from a remarkable twenty-seven applicants: Anna Longrigg (to be known as Anna L), Siobhan Allman, Alexandru Vilcu and, starting in May, Michael Nugent (who began an academic term in January). These co-op students brought incredible intelligence, focus, and drive to the project, each taking a major principal responsibility—Anna L for the plaster casts, Siobhan for the moulds and photographs, and Alexandru for the production of the matrix and drawings—and each happily pitching in wherever else a brain or hands were needed.

I write these notes two weeks before we'll end production at Waterloo Architecture, six weeks before we'll begin assembly in Venice, and three months before the inauguration of *The Evidence Room*. The enthusiasm about *The Evidence Room* continues to grow, particularly now that our participation in the Biennale has been officially announced. Last Tuesday, the day of our weekly coordination meeting, I entered the studio at 9:00 a.m., to a beehive of activity: Anne and Anna B were discussing the most recent casting, Anna L was stirring a bucket of plaster, Siobhan walked in with a new mould for the casting of a crematorium blueprint, Alexandru was reviewing a spreadsheet of the weights and measures of the pieces to be shipped, and Piper was on the telephone with the shippers. The walls were filled with Donald's meticulous plans and the schedule of major and minor deadlines. And everywhere in the studio were racks of plaster casts—drawings, photos, letters...in short, evidence.

At 9:15 a.m. Michael and his father, Tom, arrived: Michael taking a break from his classes and Tom attending as our engineering consultant, advising on everything from the drying time of plaster to the stability of the matrix. Donald's car pulled up outside the studio and he and Sascha alighted and began to unload bags of plaster bought that morning in Toronto. It was bitter cold and I hurried to the Melville Café to do what I am best at: buying a big thermos of coffee. By the time I returned to the studio with what my Dutch family refer to as a *bakkie troost* (cup of consolation), all present were ready to meet and to review progress.

As the team sat down, I walked to the school's workshop, saw Bradley bent in deep concentration over the gastight door he was assembling, tapped on his shoulder, and told him it was time. "I am ready," he said, and together we walked back to the studio and joined the others at the table.

February 27, 2016

# Contributor biographies

– Siobhan Allman is an undergraduate student at the University of Waterloo School of Architecture. She was raised as an Irish-Canadian in Ottawa, Ontario. Siobhan has been employed as a machinist in San Francisco, California; a graphic designer in New York City; and an architectural intern in Toronto. With interests in fabrication and graphics, Siobhan aspires to be a polymath in the design field. She enjoys woodworking, sketching, and writing.

– Piper Bernbaum is a recent graduate from the Master of Architecture program at the University of Waterloo. Her interests centre on the appropriation of space through design, where architecture is an apparatus by which people are the constituents and subjects of making. Focused on design that addresses public interest and social conflicts, Piper's research has involved her in many community-based projects, working in Canada, Italy, Germany, France, the USA, and the Arctic.

– Anna Beznogova received her Bachelor of Architectural Studies from the University of Waterloo in 2013 and is completing her Master of Architecture at the same institution. Anna has had a lifelong interest in craft, which is how she became involved with casting in various media. Her work revolves around the notion that craft elicits an empathic response to context and material, and is a mode of meaningful work that requires tactile skill and ingenuity. Anna is applying this concept to a review of material sustainability in her master's thesis.

– Anne Bordeleau is Associate Professor at the School of Architecture of the University of Waterloo, Canada. She is an architect and historian with publications on the temporal dimensions of casting, drawings, maps, buildings, and architecture more generally. She has published articles in numerous international journals (*Journal of Architecture, Architectural Theory Review, Architectural History, Architecture_MPS, Footprint*), chapters in edited books, and a monograph, *Charles Robert Cockerell, Architect in Time: Reflections Around Anachronistic Drawings* (Ashgate, 2014).

– Elly Gotz is a graduate electronics engineer and a businessman. Born in Lithuania, he spent his teenage years in a Nazi ghetto there and later in the Dachau concentration camp, where he was liberated in 1945 by the American army. After the war he lived in Germany, Norway, Zimbabwe, and South Africa. Elly came to Canada with his family in 1964 and lives in Toronto. He is now a regular speaker at schools and universities, where he teaches tolerance by talking about his experiences in the Holocaust. He is anxious to explain the tragedy that befell the Jewish people in Europe.

– Sascha Hastings is an independent arts producer, curator, and editor. She graduated from Albert-Ludwigs-Universität Freiburg in German Literature and has worked as a CBC Radio producer on *The Arts Tonight, The Next Chapter, Writers & Company*, and *Wachtel on the Arts*. She was the inaugural curator of Cambridge Galleries Design at Riverside, and worked on the Canada Pavilion at the 2010, 2012, and 2014 Venice Architecture Biennales. Her publications include *Logotopia: The Library in Architecture, Art and the Imagination* (2008).

– Louis-Charles Lasnier is trained as a graphic designer and architect. He worked for three highly respected firms—Bruce Mau Design, Claude Cormier landscape architects, and Saucier+Perrotte Architects—before starting his own practice in 2001. His studio was a centre for collaboration between the different design disciplines with a focus on publishing, exhibition design, and signage projects. In 2012, he joined l'École de Design de l'Université du Québec à Montréal as a full-time faculty member.

– Anna Longrigg is a fourth-year architecture student at the University of Waterloo. Through her studies and personal endeavours, she has developed an interest in how design is experienced on the human, tactile scale. With an interest in craft, materiality, and analogue methods of production, Anna has pursued work in both architectural and textile design. This interest in craft brought Anna to be primarily involved in the process of plaster casting for *The Evidence Room*.

– Donald McKay is Associate Professor at Waterloo Architecture. Before graduating (Toronto, B. Arch, 1973), McKay was an organizer in community housing. After graduation, McKay worked as an architect and planner for George Baird and for Barton Myers, and as a management consultant, renovating six of Toronto's public libraries. *Workspheres: Design and Contemporary Work Styles* (MOMA, 2001) includes McKay's furniture. His papers include "Cosmopolitan Mechanics and the Dissolution of National Boundaries" (1991), "Sanctuary" (1988), and "Logistics and Friction" in *Metropolitan Mutations* (1989). He co-authored, with Robert Jan van Pelt, "Building from Sea to Shining Sea: The Architect in North America," in *Der Architekt* (2012).

– Michael Nugent comes from a family of doers and craftsmen, as well as a lot of teachers in several forms. He has spent most of his life building, working with his father and others to refine the craft of various media, especially metal and wood. He came to architecture because he cared about how the built world supports and fosters daily life and the places in which people live. He is now studying the craft of spaces for life.

– Tom Nugent has the best job in the world. He's Michael's dad.

– Bradley Paddock is a carpenter and Master of Architecture candidate at the University of Waterloo. A historic granite and limestone double house on the banks of the Grand River in Cambridge, Ontario currently serves as a laboratory for his cross-disciplinary thesis research and marks a return to the building site where his architectural education began.

– Robert Jan van Pelt was born in the Netherlands and has taught at the University of Waterloo School of Architecture since 1987. Having earned his doctorate on the basis of a dissertation about the cosmic speculations on the Temple of Solomon, the focus of his subsequent research has been the (architectural) history of Auschwitz in particular and the history of the Holocaust in general. He has been active in the struggle against Holocaust denial.

– Alexandru Vilcu is an undergraduate candidate currently in his final term at the School of Architecture of the University of Waterloo. He has developed a strong interest in the relationship between architecture and privacy in the state of our massively surveilled world. Architecture's intrinsic value as physical evidence of intangible political ideologies kindled his interest in the translation of the Auschwitz drawing sets into casts.

Credits

The Team:

Anne Bordeleau: Principal
Sascha Hastings: Principal
Donald McKay: Principal
Robert Jan van Pelt: Principal

Siobhan Allman: Undergraduate Associate
Fysal Amirzada: Undergraduate Assistant
Piper Bernbaum: Graduate Associate
Anna Beznogova: Graduate Associate
Quinn Greer: Graduate Assistant
Carol Kaifosh: Graduate Assistant
Louis-Charles Lasnier: Graduate Assistant and Book Designer
Anna Longrigg: Undergraduate Associate
Michael Nugent: Undergraduate Associate
Bradley Paddock: Graduate Associate
Nicole Ratajczak: Undergraduate Assistant
Jake Read: Undergraduate Assistant
Patrick Verkley: Graduate Assistant
Alexandru Vilcu: Undergraduate Associate

Elly Gotz: Historical Consultant
Miriam Greenbaum: Historical Consultant
Ian Hill: Envoy-at-Large
Bob Intini: Manufacturing Consultant
Andrea Fochs Knight: Co-Publisher (New Jewish Press)
Bruce Kuwabara: Envoy-at-Large
Guan Lee: Casting Consultant
Malcolm Lester: Co-Publisher (New Jewish Press)
MCM 2001: Exhibition Matrix Manufacturer
Tom Nugent: Student Mentor and Team Advisor
Marwan Osseiran: Envoy-at-Large
Joy Roberts: Envoy-at-Large
Sandra Simpson: Envoy-at-Large
Paul Socken: Envoy-at-Large
Jean-Jacques van Vlasselaer: Envoy-at-Large
Carol Weinbaum: Envoy-at-Large

Donors:

Presenting Donor:
 The Gerald Schwartz & Heather Reisman Foundation

Principal Donor:
 The Azrieli Foundation

Major Donors:
 Bocci
 Bob Intini
 KPMB Architects
 Mark and Lindy Mandelbaum
 Florence Minz
 David Mirvish
 Tom Nugent
 Ontario Association of Architects
 Bernadette Rosenstadt
 Sandra Simpson
 The Social Sciences and Humanities Research Council of Canada
 The University of Waterloo
 The Jack Weinbaum Family Foundation
 Tom and Sasha Weisz
 Jonathan and Susan Wener

Supporting Donors:
 Anneke Boot
 DHL Global Forwarding
 EBHW Architecture
 Elizabeth English
 Miriam Greenbaum
 Marwan Osseiran
 Stephen Otto
 Phidon Pens Limited
 Joy Roberts and Doug McMullen
 Royal Architectural Institute of Canada
 Allan Teramura
 Robert Jan van Pelt

Credits (Continued)

Collaborators (ex officio) within the University of Waterloo:
Mike den Haan: Associate Vice-President, Principal Gifts
Fred Hunsberger: Multi Media Specialist, School of Architecture
Sarah Nichols: Academic Administrative Manager, School of Architecture
Bonnie Oberle: Associate Director, Leadership Giving
Mona Skuterud: Administrative Officer, School of Architecture

Collaborating Institutions and Organizations:
The Canadian Centre for Architecture
Musealia Entertainment SL
New Jewish Press, Anne Tanenbaum Centre for Jewish Studies

With thanks to:
Enrica Abbate, Marlon Almanza, Alejandro Aravena, Tom Barber,
André Bélanger, Ilia Bélanger Bordeleau, Laure Bélanger Bordeleau,
Giovanni Bergamo, Marina Bertaggia, Shirley Blumberg, Giovanna
Borasi, Joern Brandmeyer, Wade Brown, Gerardo Cejas, George
Dixon, Nenone Donaldson, Sandra Durand de la Penne, Luis
Ferreiro, Wayne Fisher, Esmay Gotz, Erin Sargeant Greenwood,
Rick Haldenby, Feridun Hamdullahpur, Oleg Izvekov, Dan Jessel,
Heinz Kohler, Agustina Labarca, Sébastien Larivière, Delphine
Lesage, Manuela Lucà-Dazio, Manfredi Manera, Jolin Masson,
Bryan May, Eitan Mazor, Mary Misner, Sandra Montagner, Matt
Oliver, Carrie Paddock, Carlos Pallieri, Robert Papka, Wayne
Parker, Patrick Pellerin, Lorenzo Pignatti, Luigi Ricciari, Gregory
Rybak, Terry Schmidt, Lola Sheppard, Robin Simpson-McKay,
Julie Skelly, Beverley Slopen, Pearl Sullivan, Ashton Waters, Mike
Wilson, Simon Yu, Mirko Zardini, Djamel Zeniti